Problem Solvers

Edited by L. Marder
Senior Lecturer in Mathematics, University of Southampton

No. 14

Stochastic Processes

Problem Solvers

Stochastic Processes

RODNEY COLEMAN

Lecturer in Mathematics
Imperial College, University of London

LONDON · GEORGE ALLEN & UNWIN LTD
RUSKIN HOUSE   MUSEUM STREET

First published 1974

© George Allen & Unwin Ltd, 1974
ISBN 0 04 519016 X *hardback*
    0 04 519017 8 *paperback*

Set in 10 on 12 pt 'Monophoto' Times Mathematics Series 569
Printed in Great Britain by Page Bros (Norwich) Ltd., Norwich

Contents

Chapter 1
What is a Stochastic Process?

The word *stochastic* is jargon for *random*. A *stochastic process* is a system which evolves in time while undergoing chance fluctuations. We can describe such a system by defining a family of *random variables*, $\{X_t\}$, where X_t measures, at time t, the aspect of the system which is of interest. For example, X_t might be the number of customers in a queue at time t. As time passes, customers will arrive and leave, and so the value of X_t will change. At any time t, X_t takes one of the values $0, 1, 2, \ldots$; and t can be any value in a subset of $(-\infty, \infty)$, the infinite past to the infinite future. If we observe the queue continuously, and customers arrive one at a time to be served by a single server, then, when a customer arrives, the value of X_t, the queue size, increases by one, and when a customer departs after being served, X_t decreases by one (Figure 1.1). The values which X_t

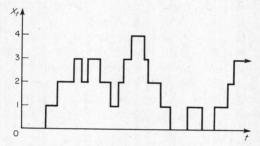

Figure 1.1 The number of customers, X_t, in a queue at time t

can take are called its *states*, and changes in the value of X_t are called *transitions* between its states. If we observe the queue size not continuously but at unit intervals, say once every quarter of an hour, then more than one customer can arrive or leave in each time interval. This will lead to larger fluctuations in the value of X_t. These obvious statements represent the basis of the construction of a model of a queue which incorporates random intervals between the arrivals of customers and random periods spent at the service point. It is the often complex consequences of these idealised models which we shall be studying. Simple as these models are, by incorporating a little of the randomness of the real world they bring us far closer to understanding the real world than could possibly be achieved with models which neglect such random behaviour.

Stochastic models are applicable to any system involving chance variability as time passes. In geophysics they have been used for the prediction of the size and whereabouts of earthquakes, in geography to study the spread of shoe shops in a growing city, in entomology the way in which aphids congregate on the leaves of plants, in nature conservancy the way in which birds, turtles and eels navigate, and in industry they have been used for the prediction of the durations of strikes.

By a *stochastic process*, we shall mean a family of random variables $\{X_t\}$, where t is a point in a space T called the *parameter space*, and where, for each $t \in T$, X_t is a point in a space S called the *state space*.

The family $\{X_t\}$ may be thought of as the path of a particle moving 'randomly' in space S, its position at time t being X_t. A record of one of these paths is called a *realisation* of the process.

We are interested in relations between the X_t for different fixed values of t. We apply the theory of probability to determine these relationships.

Other aspects of stochastic processes will also interest us. For example, the time which elapses before a gambler loses all his capital, or the chance that any customer who might enter a shop in a fixed interval $(0, t)$ will be served without having to wait. By thinking in terms of a particle travelling in a space we can often demonstrate the applicability of the same model to widely differing situations. For example, the time to a gambler's ruin, the time before a reservoir dries up, the time for the server of a queue to become free and the time before an animal population becomes extinct are all equivalent to the time before the particle first hits a point O. At that time the gambler's resources have been reduced to zero, the water level is down to zero, the number of waiting customers is zero and the population size is zero.

Problem 1.1 What are the state space and parameter space for a stochastic process which is the score during a football match?

Solution. The state space S is the set of possible values the score can take, so $S = \{(x, y) : x, y = 0, 1, 2, \ldots\}$. If we measure time in minutes, then the parameter space T is $(0, 90)$. The process starts in state $(0, 0)$, and transitions take place between the states of S whenever a goal is scored. A goal increases x or y by one, so the score (x, y) will then go to $(x+1, y)$ or $(x, y+1)$. □

Problem 1.2 Describe how we might use a stochastic process to study the resources of an insurance company.

Solution. We let the resources at time t be a random variable X_t. Then X_t will increase at a randomly fluctuating but fairly steady rate as premiums come in, but is subject to sudden falls as claims are met. □

Problem 1.3 What are the state space and parameter space for a stochastic process which is the depth of the sea in position **x** at time τ?

Solution. The depth of the sea is measured from the top of a wave down to the seabed. As the waves move about, the depth at any fixed point **x** will vary with time, regardless of any larger-scale influences such as tides. We can measure the depth at any time τ, and in any position **x**, so the parameter space T is the set of all $t = (\tau, \mathbf{x})$ for which $-\infty < \tau < \infty$ and $\mathbf{x} \in \mathcal{X}$, where $\mathcal{X}$ is the set of map references for the entire sea. Here t is not just time, but a combination of time and space coordinates. The state space S is the set of all values which the depth can possibly be, so $S = [0, \infty)$, where the depth is 0 when the seabed is exposed, and we do not limit the height the waves can reach, although a wave of infinite height will not occur without a miracle. $\square$

Problem 1.4 *An epidemic process.* A fatal disease is brought into a closed community by a single infected individual. Describe how the spread of the disease may be studied as a stochastic process.

Solution. We suppose that, for a period, infected persons show no symptoms and are not infectious. They then become carriers, and are infectious, but still show no symptoms. Carriers, after a period, exhibit symptoms of the disease and are isolated. These people are cured and become immune, or else they die.

Let M be the class of immune members of the community; S be the class of susceptibles, that is, people at risk; N be the noninfectious incubators of the disease; C, the carriers; I, the carriers who have been isolated; and D, the dead. Initially all members of the community are in M or S, except the single infected person in N or C. Transitions between classes take place only according to the arrows in Figure 1.2.

The random variables of interest are the numbers in each of the classes at each time t. The progress of the disease will depend on the degree of

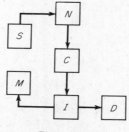

Figure 1.2

immunity, the amount of contact between carriers and susceptibles, the rate at which carriers are detected, and the chance of a cure being effected. Epidemiologists use the theory of stochastic processes to seek ways of influencing the rates of transition between the classes. ☐

Problem 1.5 *A library book loan process.* A reader visits a library regularly at the same time each week. There, if he has finished the book he is currently borrowing, he exchanges it; otherwise he has its loan renewed. Consider the stochastic process $\{Z_n : n = \ldots, -1, 0, 1, 2, \ldots\}$, where Z_n is the number of renewals of the book currently being borrowed as the reader leaves the library in week n, where the weeks are measured from an arbitrary time point.

If a book has just been exchanged, then $Z_n = 0$. What is the state space for this process, and what are the possible transitions of state?

Solution. State space S is $\{0, 1, 2, \ldots\}$, since Z_n can take any value $0, 1, 2, \ldots$; though it would have to be a massive tome for very large values. If $Z_n = k (k = 0, 1, 2, \ldots)$, then in week $n+1$ if the book being read is completed, it is exchanged and a new book is borrowed, so $Z_{n+1} = 0$. Otherwise, the loan is renewed for another week, so $Z_{n+1} = k+1$. ☐

Problem 1.6 *A dam storage process.* Consider a dam which can hold at most w units of water. Suppose that during day n, y_n units of water flow into the dam, any overflow being lost. Provided the dam is not dry, one unit of water is released at the end of each day. Suppose that $\{y_n\}$ is a sequence of nonnegative integers, and that w is a positive integer. What is the state space for $\{Z_n : n = 0, 1, 2, \ldots\}$, where Z_n is the content of the dam after the release (if any) of the unit of water on day n? Show how Z_{n+1} depends on Z_n and y_{n+1}.

Solution. If the dam is full on day n, then after the unit release, Z_n will take value $w-1$. If we then have a dry day (i.e. $y_{n+1} = 0$), $Z_{n+1} = w-2$. After another dry day ($y_{n+2} = 0$), $Z_{n+2} = w-3$; and so on, until after the $(w-1)$st dry day, $Z_{n+w-1} = 0$. Clearly these will be the only possible values that Z_n can take. The state space is therefore $\{0, 1, 2, \ldots, w-1\}$.

If $Z_n = i$ ($i = 0, 1, \ldots, w-1$) and $y_{n+1} = k$ ($k = 0, 1, 2, \ldots$), then

$$Z_{n+1} = \begin{cases} 0 & (i+k = 0 \text{ or } 1) \\ i+k-1 & (i+k = 2, 3, \ldots, w-1) \\ w-1 & (i+k = w, w+1, \ldots) \end{cases}$$ ☐

Problem 1.7 A factory has two machines, but on any given day not more than one is in use. This machine has a constant probability p of breaking down and, if it does, the breakdown occurs at the end of the day's work. A single repairman is employed. It takes him two days to repair a machine, and he works on only one machine at a time. Construct a stochastic process which will describe the working of this factory.

Solution. We must select a suitable random variable to observe. Clearly its value need be recorded only at the end of each day, since all transitions occur just before then. The parameter space T will therefore be the set of working days during which this system is in use. Let us call the first day, 1; the second, 2; and so on; then $T = \{1, 2, 3, \ldots\}$.

A suitable stochastic process is $\{X_n : n \in T\}$, where we record at the end of day n the value of X_n, the number of days that would be needed to get both machines back in working order. If both machines are in working order, then X_n is 0. If one machine is in working order and the other has already had one day's repair carried out on it, then X_n is 1. If one machine is in working order, and the other has just broken down, then X_n is 2. If one machine has just broken down, and the other has had one day's repair carried out on it, then X_n is 3. These are the only possible cases, so the state space is $S = \{0, 1, 2, 3\}$. □

EXERCISES

1.   List the set of possible transitions between the states of the factory described in Problem 1.7.

2.   Choose random variables suitable for studying the behaviour of traffic at the junction between a main road and a side road.

3.   Construct a process for studying the counting of the votes in an election fight between just two candidates.

4.   Describe the process $\{X_t\}$, where X_t is the number of teeth an individual has at time t if he was born at time $t = 0$. Clearly $X_0 = 0$.

Chapter 2
Results from Probability Theory

This chapter contains results from elementary probability theory. Those to whom this is all familiar should nevertheless read it to acquaint themselves with the notation, some of which has been introduced specifically to facilitate the study of stochastic processes, and so differs from that generally used.

2.1 Introduction to probability theory An *experiment* is any situation in which there is a set of possible outcomes. For example, a competition or game, a horse race, a ballot, a law suit are all experiments since their results are uncertain. A *random variable* (which we abbreviate to rv) is a number associated with the outcome of an experiment. For example, the experiment might be for a dentist to observe the number of natural teeth a patient has. Then the rv, X, will take value 28 if the patient has 28 teeth. An rv is called *discrete* if it can take only a finite or countably infinite number of distinct values. For example, the number of teeth must be one of the numbers 0 to 32.

Since the outcomes of an experiment are uncertain, associated with each outcome there will be a *probability*. The probability that rv X takes value x will be the probability that the outcome associated with x occurs. We write this: $\text{pr}(X = x)$. If a discrete rv, X, can take values $x_1, x_2, \ldots$ in a set S, then the sequence of numbers $p_{x_1}, p_{x_2}, \ldots$, where

$$p_x = \text{pr}(X = x) \quad (x \in S)$$

is called the *probability distribution* of the rv X, and

$$p_x > 0 \, (x \in S), \qquad \sum_{x \in S} p_x = p_{x_1} + p_{x_2} + \ldots = 1$$

For any subset S^* of S

$$\text{pr}(X \in S^*) = \sum_{x \in S^*} p_x \qquad (2.1)$$

For example, in throwing a die, if X is the value it shows, then $S = \{1, 2, 3, 4, 5, 6\}$. If the die is *fair* then $p_x = \frac{1}{6} \, (x \in S)$. To find the probability that an even number shows, we define $S^* = \{2, 4, 6\}$, then

$$\text{pr}(\text{an even number shows}) = \text{pr}(X \in S^*) = \text{pr}(X = 2 \text{ or } 4 \text{ or } 6)$$
$$= p_2 + p_4 + p_6$$

If $\text{pr}(X = x) = 0$ for every real x, then rv X is called *continuous*. For example, X might be a height or a weight. Its value will have an infinite decimal expansion, although in practice we must round off our measurements.

The *distribution function* (abbreviation: df) of an rv X is the function
$$F(x) = \text{pr}(X \leqslant x)$$
F is a nondecreasing function of x, and
$$F(-\infty) = 0, \qquad F(\infty) = 1$$
If there is a nonnegative function $f(x)$ such that we can write
$$F(x) = \int_{-\infty}^{x} f(y)\, dy$$
then
$$f(x) = \frac{dF(x)}{dx}$$
is the *probability density function* (abbreviation: density) of X, and X is continuous. For example, if rv X has an *exponential distribution* with parameter λ, then
$$F(x) = \begin{cases} 0 & (x \leqslant 0) \\ 1 - e^{-\lambda x} & (x > 0) \end{cases}, \qquad f(x) = \begin{cases} 0 & (x \leqslant 0) \\ \lambda e^{-\lambda x} & (x > 0) \end{cases} \qquad (2.2)$$
We write: X is $\mathscr{E}(\lambda)$.

We can interpret the density as a probability by writing
$$f(x)\, dx = \text{pr}\{X \in (x, x + dx)\}$$

If X is an rv, then so is $\psi(X)$ for any real-valued function ψ. If X is discrete, then so also is $\psi(X)$, and we define the *expectation* (or *expected value*) of $\psi(X)$ by
$$\text{E}\,\psi(X) = \sum_{x \in S} \psi(x)\text{pr}(X = x) \qquad (2.3)$$
Similarly, if X is continuous, the expectation of $\psi(X)$ is
$$\text{E}\,\psi(X) = \int_{-\infty}^{\infty} \psi(x)f(x)\, dx \qquad (2.4)$$

The expectation of X, $\text{E}X$, is called the *mean* of the distribution of X, and is generally denoted by μ. By taking $\psi(x) = ax + b$, where a and b are constants and expanding the right sides of equations 2.3 and 2.4, we find that
$$\text{E}(aX + b) = a\,\text{E}X + b \qquad (2.5)$$
The *variance* of the distribution of X, $\text{V}X$, is defined as $\text{E}(X - \mu)^2$, where $\mu = \text{E}X$, and is generally denoted by σ^2. We can write $\text{V}X$ in the convenient form
$$\text{V}X = \text{E}X^2 - (\text{E}X)^2 \qquad (2.6)$$

7

Problem 2.1   If rv X is $\mathscr{E}(\lambda)$, find EX, VX.

Solution. From equations 2.2 and 2.4,

$$EX = \int_0^\infty x\lambda e^{-\lambda x}\, dx = 1/\lambda$$

$$EX^2 = \int_0^\infty x^2 \lambda e^{-\lambda x}\, dx = 2/\lambda^2$$

Therefore

$$VX = \frac{2}{\lambda^2} - \left(\frac{1}{\lambda}\right)^2 = \frac{1}{\lambda^2} \qquad \square$$

Problem 2.2   Find EX and VX if rv X has the *Bernoulli distribution* with parameter θ.

Solution. We write: X is $\mathscr{B}(\theta)$. The parameter is called the *probability of success*, since the Bernoulli distribution is often used as a model for experiments which have only two outcomes: *success* and *failure*. If the outcome is success we set $X = 1$, if failure then $X = 0$. Other applications are when the outcomes are *on* and *off*, *yes* and *no*, or *heads* and *tails*. The probability distribution of X is therefore

$$\mathrm{pr}(X = 1) = \theta, \qquad \mathrm{pr}(X = 0) = 1 - \theta$$

From equations 2.3 and 2.6

$$EX = 1 \times \mathrm{pr}(X = 1) + 0 \times \mathrm{pr}(X = 0) = \mathrm{pr}(X = 1) = \theta \qquad (2.7)$$

$$EX^2 = 1^2 \times \mathrm{pr}(X = 1) + 0^2 \times \mathrm{pr}(X = 0) = \theta$$

Therefore

$$VX = EX^2 - (EX)^2 = \theta - \theta^2 = \theta(1 - \theta) \qquad \square$$

Problem 2.3   Construct a model for the experiment in which a fair coin is tossed n times.

Solution. Consider the experiment, or *trial*, in which a coin is tossed just once. Then the large experiment is a sequence of n of these trials. The outcome of a trial can be either 'a head shows' or 'a tail shows'. We shall label these H and T respectively, as a convenient abbreviation. Then, since the coin is fair, $\mathrm{pr}(H) = \mathrm{pr}(T) = \frac{1}{2}$. Let us define an rv X which takes value 1 if H, and value 0 if T. Then X is $\mathscr{B}(\frac{1}{2})$. The trial is called a *Bernoulli trial*.

Now suppose that we repeat this trial n times under identical conditions; that is, we carry out a sequence of n independent Bernoulli trials. (Independence will be defined formally later.) We then define rvs

$$X_k = \begin{cases} 1 & \text{if } H \text{ on } k\text{th trial} \\ 0 & \text{if } T \text{ on } k\text{th trial} \end{cases} \qquad (k = 1, 2, \ldots, n)$$

where each X_k is independently $\mathscr{B}(\frac{1}{2})$. The sequence of rvs $X_1, X_2, \ldots, X_n$

8

describes the coin-tossing experiment. □

If we are interested in the number of heads that will be observed in the experiment, we define rv

$$Z_n = X_1 + \ldots + X_n$$

which, as the sequence of trials proceeds, increases by one every time the coin comes down head uppermost. We note that as n increases, sequence $\{Z_n\}$ is a stochastic process. It is a very important process, being the basis for random walk models.

2.2 Bivariate distributions The *joint distribution function* of a pair (X, Y) of rvs is the function $F_{X,Y}$ of two real variables defined by

$$F(x, y) = F_{X,Y}(x, y) = \text{pr}(X \leqslant x, \quad Y \leqslant y)$$

It is the probability that the value of rv X does not exceed x and the value of rv Y does not exceed y. The subscripts will be used when we wish to avoid ambiguity; for example, in Section 2.1 for the rv X we could have used f_X, F_X, μ_X, σ_X^2, E_X, V_X. For (X, Y),

$$F(x, \infty) = \text{pr}(X \leqslant x, \quad Y \leqslant \infty) = \text{pr}(X \leqslant x) = F_X(x) \qquad (2.8)$$

is called the *marginal distribution* of X. If

$$F(x, \infty)F(\infty, y) = F(x, y) \qquad (2.9)$$

for every (x, y), then rvs X and Y are said to be *independent*.

If X and Y are discrete rvs which take values in sets S_X and S_Y respectively, then, from equation 2.8, the marginal distribution of X is

$$\text{pr}(X = x) = \sum_{y \in S_Y} \text{pr}(X = x, \quad Y = y) \quad (x \in S_X) \qquad (2.10)$$

The *conditional probability* that X takes value x, given that Y has taken value $y \in S_Y$, is defined by

$$\text{pr}(X = x \mid Y = y) = \frac{\text{pr}(X = x, \quad Y = y)}{\text{pr}(Y = y)} \qquad (2.11)$$

From equation 2.10, therefore,

$$\text{pr}(X = x) = \sum_{y \in S_Y} \text{pr}(X = x \mid Y = y)\text{pr}(Y = y) \qquad (2.12)$$

A conditional distribution has all the properties of a probability distribution, and so we can define the expectation of X given that $Y = y$,

$$E_{X|Y=y} X = \sum_{x \in S_X} x \, \text{pr}(X = x \mid Y = y)$$

If X and Y are independent, then, from equation 2.9,

9

$$\text{pr}(X = x, \quad Y = y) = \text{pr}(X = x)\text{pr}(Y = y) \quad \text{(for } \textit{every } x \in S_X, \quad y \in S_Y)$$

and so, from equation 2.11,

$$\text{pr}(X = x \mid Y = y) = \text{pr}(X = x)$$

A joint df $F_{X,Y}$ has a density if there is a nonnegative function $f_{X,Y}$ of two real variables such that for every (x, y)

$$F_{X,Y}(x, y) = \int_{-\infty}^{x} \int_{-\infty}^{y} f_{X,Y}(u, v) \, dv \, du$$

Then

$$f_{X,Y}(x, y) \, dx \, dy = \text{pr}\{X \in (x, x + dx), \quad Y \in (y, y + dy)\}$$

The *marginal density* of X is

$$f_X(x) = \int_{-\infty}^{\infty} f_{X,Y}(x, y) \, dy$$

The *conditional density* of X given $Y = y$ is

$$f_{X|Y=y}(x) = \frac{f_{X,Y}(x, y)}{f_Y(y)} \quad \text{(if } f_Y(y) > 0) \tag{2.13}$$

The value y is given and so is a known constant. The expectation of X given $Y = y$ is

$$E_{X|Y=y} X = \int_{-\infty}^{\infty} x f_{X|Y=y}(x) \, dx \tag{2.14}$$

If X and Y are independent then, from equation 2.9,

$$f_{X,Y}(x, y) = f_X(x) f_Y(y) \quad \text{for every } (x, y) \tag{2.15}$$

so, from equation 2.13,

$$f_{X|Y=y}(x) = f_X(x) \tag{2.16}$$

Now

$$E_{X,Y} \psi(X, Y) = \int_{-\infty}^{\infty} \int_{-\infty}^{\infty} \psi(x, y) f_{X,Y}(x, y) \, dx \, dy \tag{2.17}$$

or

$$\sum_{x \in S_X} \sum_{y \in S_Y} \psi(x, y) \text{pr}(X = x, \quad Y = y)$$

We define the *covariance* of rvs X and Y to be

$$\text{cov}(X, Y) = E_{X,Y}\{(X - E_{X,Y} X)(Y - E_{X,Y} Y)\}$$
$$= E_{X,Y}(XY) - (E_X X)(E_Y Y) \tag{2.18}$$

Problem 2.4 Bivariate rv (X, Y) takes values $(-2, 4), (-1, 1), (1, 1), (2, 4)$, each with probability $\frac{1}{4}$. (i) Find the marginal distributions of X and Y, and calculate $\text{cov}(X, Y)$. (ii) Show that X and Y are not independent.

10

Solution. (i) The marginal distributions of X and Y are:
$$\text{pr}(X = -2) = \text{pr}(X = -2, \quad Y = 4) = \tfrac{1}{4}$$
$$\text{pr}(X = -1) = \text{pr}(X = 1) = \text{pr}(X = 2) = \tfrac{1}{4}$$
similarly;
$$\text{pr}(Y = 1) = \text{pr}\{(X = -1, \quad Y = 1)\text{or}(X = 1, \quad Y = 1)\} = \tfrac{1}{4} + \tfrac{1}{4} = \tfrac{1}{2}$$
$$\text{pr}(Y = 4) = \tfrac{1}{2}$$
similarly,
$$\text{E}X = \tfrac{1}{4}\{(-2) + (-1) + 1 + 2\} = 0, \qquad \text{E}Y = \tfrac{1}{2}(1 + 4) = \tfrac{5}{2}$$
and
$$\text{E}(XY) = \tfrac{1}{4}\{(-2 \times 4) + (-1 \times 1) + (1 \times 1) + (2 \times 4)\} = 0.$$
Therefore
$$\text{cov}(X, Y) = \text{E}(XY) - (\text{E}X)(\text{E}Y) = 0$$
(ii) $\quad 0 = \text{pr}(X = -2, \quad Y = 1) \neq \text{pr}(X = -2)\text{pr}(Y = 1) = \tfrac{1}{4} \times \tfrac{1}{2} = \tfrac{1}{8}$

Therefore, X and Y are not independent. We note that $Y = X^2$. $\quad\square$
If X and Y are both continuous rvs, from equations 2.17 and 2.13,
$$\text{E}_{X,Y}\psi(X, Y) = \int_{-\infty}^{\infty} \int_{-\infty}^{\infty} \psi(x, y) f_{X|Y=y}(x) f_Y(y) \, dx \, dy$$
$$= \int_{-\infty}^{\infty} \left\{ \int_{-\infty}^{\infty} \psi(x, y) f_{X|Y=y}(x) dx \right\} f_Y(y) \, dy = \text{E}_Y\{\text{E}_{X|Y=Y} \psi(X, Y)\}$$
Similarly, if one or other or both of X and Y is discrete,
$$\text{E}_{X,Y}\psi(X, Y) = \text{E}_Y \text{E}_{X|Y=Y} \psi(X, Y) \tag{2.19}$$
This will be called the *decomposition rule* and is the most important single device we shall use in our treatment of stochastic processes. For example, if $\{Z_n\}$ is the path of a particle, then to determine $\text{E}\psi(Z_n)$ we can condition on the position $Z_k \ (k < n)$ at an earlier time, i.e.
$$\text{E}\psi(Z_n) = \text{E}_{Z_k, Z_n} \psi(Z_n) = \text{E}_{Z_k} \text{E}_{Z_n|Z_k = Z_k} \psi(Z_n) \tag{2.20}$$
A special case of equation 2.19 is when ψ depends only on X. Then
$$\text{E}_{X,Y}\psi(X) = \text{E}_X \text{E}_{Y|X=x} \psi(X) = \text{E}_X \psi(X) \tag{2.21}$$
since, given $X = X$, $\psi(X)$ is a constant, so
$$\text{E}_{Y|X=x} \psi(X) = \psi(X)$$
This result was used in equation 2.18.

Problem 2.5 If the distribution of $X \mid Y = y$ is $\mathscr{B}(\theta(y))$, show that the marginal distribution of X is $\mathscr{B}(\text{E}_Y \theta(Y))$.

Solution. From equation 2.7,
$$\text{E}_{X|Y=y} X = \text{pr}(X = 1 \mid Y = y) = \theta(y)$$

Therefore
$$\text{pr}(X = 1) = E_X X = E_Y E_{X|Y=Y} X = E_Y \theta(Y)$$
Clearly X can take only 2 values, 0 and 1; therefore
$$\text{pr}(X = 0) = 1 - \text{pr}(X = 1) = 1 - E_Y \theta(Y)$$
so rv X is $\mathscr{B}(E_Y \theta(Y))$. ☐

Problem 2.6 Show that
$$V_{X,Y} \psi(X, Y) = E_Y V_{X|Y=Y} \psi(X, Y) + V_Y E_{X|Y=Y} \psi(X, Y) \qquad (2.22)$$
Solution. We shall abbreviate $\psi(X, Y)$ to ψ. By equation 2.6,

$$
\begin{aligned}
V_{X,Y} \psi &= E_{X,Y} \psi^2 - (E_{X,Y} \psi)^2 \\
&= \{E_Y E_{X|Y=Y} \psi^2 - E_Y (E_{X|Y=Y} \psi)^2\} \\
&\qquad\qquad + \{E_Y (E_{X|Y=Y} \psi)^2 - (E_Y E_{X|Y=Y} \psi)^2\} \\
&= E_Y V_{X|Y=Y} \psi + V_Y E_{X|Y=Y} \psi
\end{aligned}
$$

where we used equation 2.19 and introduced two middle terms which cancel. ☐

Problem 2.7 Show that if X and Y are independent rvs, then for any real-valued functions ϕ and ψ
$$E_{X,Y}\{\phi(X)\psi(Y)\} = \{E_X \phi(X)\} \{E_Y \psi(Y)\}$$

Solution. By equations 2.14 and 2.16
$$E_{X|Y=y} \phi(X) = E_X \phi(X)$$

also
$$E_{X,Y}\{\phi(X)\psi(Y)\} = E_Y E_{X|Y=Y}\{\phi(X)\psi(Y)\} = E_Y \psi(Y) E_{X|Y=Y} \phi(X)$$
by equation 2.5, since, given $Y = Y$, $\psi(Y)$ is a constant. Therefore
$$E_{X,Y}\{\phi(X)\psi(Y)\} = E_Y \psi(Y)\{E_X \phi(X)\} = \{E_X \phi(X)\} \{E_Y \psi(Y)\}$$
since, with respect to the marginal distribution of Y, $E_X \phi(X)$ is a constant. ☐

2.3 Multivariate distributions

Rvs $X_1, \ldots, X_n$ are *mutually independent* if, for every subset, $X_{i_1}, \ldots, X_{i_k}$, of two or more,

$$\text{pr}(X_{i_1} \leqslant x_1, \quad \ldots, \quad X_{i_k} \leqslant x_k) = \text{pr}(X_{i_1} \leqslant x_1)\ldots\text{pr}(X_{i_k} \leqslant x_k)$$
$$\text{for every } (x_1, \ldots, x_k)$$

We can extend the definition of conditional probability to show, for example, that if $Y_1, \ldots, Y_n$ are discrete rvs then
$$\text{pr}(Y_1 = y_1, \quad \ldots, \quad Y_n = y_n)$$

$$= \mathrm{pr}(Y_1 = y_1)\mathrm{pr}(Y_2 = y_2 \mid Y_1 = y_1)\mathrm{pr}(Y_3 = y_3 \mid Y_1 = y_1, \quad Y_2 = y_2)$$
$$\ldots \mathrm{pr}(Y_n = y_n \mid Y_1 = y_1, \quad \ldots, \quad Y_{n-1} = y_{n-1}) \qquad (2.23)$$

From this we can generalise the decomposition rule to

$$\mathrm{E}_{Y_1,\ldots,Y_n}\psi(Y_1,\ldots,Y_n) = \mathrm{E}_{Y_1}\mathrm{E}_{Y_2|Y_1=Y_1}\mathrm{E}_{Y_3|Y_1=Y_1,Y_2=Y_2}$$
$$\ldots \mathrm{E}_{Y_n|Y_1=Y_1,\ldots,Y_{n-1}=Y_{n-1}}\psi(Y_1,\ldots,Y_n).$$

The result of Problem 2.7 generalises.

Problem 2.8 Show that if $X_1, \ldots, X_n$ are independently distributed rvs, then

$$B_n = \mathrm{E}_{X_1,\ldots,X_n}\{\psi_1(X_1)\ldots\psi_n(X_n)\} = \{\mathrm{E}_{X_1}\psi_1(X_1)\}\ldots\{\mathrm{E}_{X_n}\psi_n(X_n)\}$$
$$= A_1 A_2 \ldots A_n, \quad \text{say}$$

Solution. We use the method of induction. By Problem 2.7

$$B_2 = A_1 A_2$$

Suppose

$$B_{n-1} = A_1 A_2 \ldots A_{n-1}$$

Then, since $X_1, \ldots, X_n$ are independent,

$$\mathrm{E}_{X_1,\ldots,X_{n-1}|X_n=x}\,\phi(X_1,\ldots,X_{n-1})\psi(X_n) = \mathrm{E}_{X_1,\ldots,X_{n-1}}\,\phi(X_1,\ldots,X_{n-1})\psi(x)$$
$$= \psi(x)\mathrm{E}_{X_1,\ldots,X_{n-1}}\,\phi(X_1,\ldots,X_{n-1})$$

Therefore

$$B_n = \mathrm{E}_{X_n}\mathrm{E}_{X_1,\ldots,X_{n-1}|X_n=X_n}\{\psi_1(X_1)\ldots\psi_n(X_n)\}$$
$$= \{\mathrm{E}_{X_n}\psi_n(X_n)\}\mathrm{E}_{X_1,\ldots,X_{n-1}}\{\psi_1(X_1)\ldots\psi_{n-1}(X_{n-1})\} = A_n B_{n-1}$$
$$= A_n(A_1 A_2 \ldots A_{n-1})$$

The result is thus proved. □

The converse is not necessarily true. In Problem 2.4 we had rvs X and Y which were not independent, but for which

$$\mathrm{E}_{X,Y}(XY) = (\mathrm{E}_X X)(\mathrm{E}_Y Y)$$

In a stochastic process $\{X_n\}$ the states of the system, $X_1, X_2, \ldots$ will in general not be independent, and we shall deal with consequences of this. In particular we shall study the special case in which X_n depends on X_{n-1}, but not on $X_{n-2}, X_{n-3}, \ldots$.

2.4 Probability generating functions If X is an rv having discrete distribution $p_k = \mathrm{pr}(X = x_k)\,(k = 0, 1, 2, \ldots)$, then the *probability generating function* (abbreviated to pgf) of the distribution of X is

$$G(s) = \mathrm{E}_X s^X = \sum_{k=0}^{\infty} p_k s^{x_k}$$

13

Now
$$G(1) = 1, \qquad G'(1) = \frac{dG(s)}{ds}\bigg|_{s=1} = EX, \qquad G''(1) = E\{X(X-1)\}$$

so
$$EX = G'(1), \qquad VX = G''(1) + G'(1) - \{G'(1)\}^2 \qquad (2.24)$$

Problem 2.9 Find the pgf for an rv X which is $\mathcal{B}(\theta)$.

Solution. $\mathrm{pr}(X = 1) = \theta$, $\mathrm{pr}(X = 0) = 1-\theta$. Therefore
$$G(s) = (1-\theta)s^0 + \theta s^1 = 1-\theta+\theta s \qquad \square$$

Problem 2.10 Find the pgf for an rv X which has a *Poisson distribution* with parameter λ.

Solution. We write that X is $\mathcal{P}(\lambda)$. Here
$$p_k = \mathrm{pr}(X = k) = \frac{\lambda^k e^{-\lambda}}{k!} \quad (k = 0,1,2,\ldots)$$

where $k! = 1 \times 2 \times 3 \times \ldots \times k$, and, by convention, $0! = 1$. Then
$$G(s) = \sum_{k=0}^{\infty} p_k s^k = \sum_{k=0}^{\infty} \frac{\lambda^k e^{-\lambda}}{k!} s^k = e^{-\lambda} \sum_{k=0}^{\infty} \frac{(\lambda s)^k}{k!} = e^{-\lambda} e^{\lambda s} = e^{-\lambda(1-s)}$$
$$(2.25) \qquad \square$$

Problem 2.11 Find the pgf for an rv X which has a *binomial distribution* with parameters n and θ.

Solution. We write that X is $\mathrm{Bin}(n, \theta)$. Here
$$p_k = \mathrm{pr}(X = k) = \binom{n}{k} \theta^k (1-\theta)^{n-k} \quad (k = 0,1,\ldots,n) \qquad (2.26)$$

where
$$\binom{n}{k} = \frac{n!}{k!(n-k)!}$$

So
$$G(s) = \sum_{k=0}^{n} p_k s^k = \sum_{k=0}^{n} \binom{n}{k} \theta^k (1-\theta)^{n-k} s^k = \sum_{k=0}^{n} \binom{n}{k} (\theta s)^k (1-\theta)^{n-k}$$
$$= \{\theta s + (1-\theta)\}^n \quad \text{(by the binomial theorem)}$$
$$= (1-\theta+\theta s)^n \qquad \square \quad (2.27)$$

Problem 2.12 Prove that if rvs $X_1, \ldots, X_n$ are mutually independent, and if X_k has pgf $G_k(s)$ ($k = 1, 2, \ldots, n$), then rv $Z_n = X_1 + \ldots + X_n$ has pgf

14

$$H_n(s) = \prod_{k=1}^{n} G_k(s).$$

Solution.

$$H_n(s) = E_{Z_n} s^{Z_n} = E_{X_1,\dots,X_n} s^{X_1+\dots+X_n} = E_{X_1} s^{X_1} \dots E_{X_n} s^{X_n} = \prod_{k=1}^{n} G_k(s)$$

by Problem 2.8. $\qquad\qquad\blacksquare$

As a consequence, if X_k is $\mathscr{P}(\lambda_k)$, then Z_n is $\mathscr{P}\left(\sum_{k=1}^{n} \lambda_k\right)$ (from equation 2.25); and if X_k is $\mathrm{Bin}(m_k, \theta)$ then Z_n is $\mathrm{Bin}\left(\sum_{k=1}^{n} m_k, \theta\right)$ (from equation 2.27). For the coin-tossing Problem 2.3 we may treat Z_n as though it were $X_1 + \dots + X_n$, where the Xs are independently $\mathscr{B}(\theta)$, i.e. independently $\mathrm{Bin}(1, \theta)$.

Problem 2.13 If the conditional distribution of rv X, given that $N = n$, is $\mathrm{Bin}(n, \theta)$, and if N is $\mathrm{Bin}(m, \alpha)$, what is the marginal distribution of X?

Solution. By equation 2.27,

$$G_{X|N=n}(s) = E_{X|N=n} s^X = (1-\theta+\theta s)^n$$

and

$$G_N(w) = E_N w^N = (1-\alpha+\alpha w)^m$$

Therefore

$$G_X(s) = E_X s^X = E_{X,N} s^X = E_N E_{X|N=N} s^X \quad \text{(by equation 2.21)}$$
$$= E_N (1-\theta+\theta s)^N = G_N(1-\theta+\theta s) = \{1-\alpha+\alpha(1-\theta+\theta s)\}^m$$
$$= (1-\alpha\theta+\alpha\theta s)^m$$

We recognise that this is the pgf of a $\mathrm{Bin}(m, \alpha\theta)$ rv. $\qquad\qquad\blacksquare$

Problem 2.14 If X_1, X_2, ... is a sequence of independent rvs, each having pgf $G(s)$, find the pgf for $Z_N = X_1 + X_2 + \dots + X_N$, where N is an rv having pgf $H(s)$.

Solution. By Problem 2.12

$$E_{Z_N|N=n} s^{Z_N} = E_{Z_n} s^{Z_n} = \{G(s)\}^n$$

Therefore

$$E_{Z_N} s^{Z_N} = E_N E_{Z_N|N=N} s^{Z_N} = E_N \{G(s)\}^N = H\{G(s)\}$$

since

$$H(s) = E_N s^N. \qquad\qquad\blacksquare$$

Problem 2.13 is a special case of Problem 2.14 in which the X_k are independently $\mathscr{B}(\theta)$ rvs.

15

2.5 Characteristic functions The *characteristic function* (abbreviated to cf) for an rv X is

$$\phi(\theta) = \mathrm{E}_X e^{i\theta X} \quad (i = \sqrt{(-1)}, \quad -\infty < \theta < \infty)$$

There is a one–one relationship between the df F and the cf ϕ for a rv X. If X is a discrete rv having pgf G, then

$$\phi(\theta) = \mathrm{E}(e^{i\theta})^X = G(e^{i\theta})$$

so the techniques developed in problems about pgfs can also be used with cfs. For example, as in Problem 2.12, if $X_1, \ldots, X_n$ are independent rvs having cfs $\phi_1(\theta), \ldots, \phi_n(\theta)$ respectively, then $Z_n = X_1 + \ldots + X_n$ has cf $\{\phi_1(\theta)\ldots\phi_n(\theta)\}$. Also, as in Problem 2.14, if $X_1, X_2, \ldots$ is a sequence of independent rvs each having cf $\phi(\theta)$, then the cf for $Z_N = X_1 + \ldots + X_N$, where N is a rv having pgf $H(s)$ is

$$\mathrm{E} e^{i\theta Z_N} = \mathrm{E}_N \{\phi(\theta)\}^N = H\{\phi(\theta)\} \tag{2.28}$$

The moments of the distribution of a rv X are given by

$$\phi(0) = 1, \qquad \phi'(0) = \frac{d\phi(\theta)}{d\theta}\bigg|_{\theta=0} = i\,\mathrm{E}X, \qquad \phi''(0) = -\mathrm{E}X^2$$

so

$$\mathrm{E}X = -i\,\phi'(0), \qquad \mathrm{V}X = -\phi''(0) + \{\phi'(0)\}^2$$

Problem 2.15 Suppose that $\mu = \mathrm{E}X$ and $\sigma^2 = \mathrm{V}X$, and define rv $Y = (X - \mu)/\sigma$. Then $\mathrm{E}Y = 0$ and $\mathrm{V}Y = 1$. Find the relationship between ϕ_X and ϕ_Y.

Solution. We can write $X = \mu + \sigma Y$, so

$$\phi_X(\theta) = \mathrm{E}_X e^{i\theta X} = \mathrm{E}_Y e^{i\theta(\mu + \sigma Y)} = e^{i\theta\mu}\mathrm{E}_Y e^{i\theta\sigma Y} = e^{i\theta\mu}\phi_Y(\theta\sigma) \qquad \square$$

This result enables us to determine ϕ_X from the often well-known standard form ϕ_Y.

Problem 2.16 Find the cf for the rv X which has a *normal distribution* with parameters μ and σ^2, i.e. having density

$$f_X(x; \mu, \sigma^2) = \frac{1}{\sqrt{(2\pi\sigma^2)}} \exp\left\{-\frac{(x-\mu)^2}{2\sigma^2}\right\} \quad (-\infty < x < \infty) \tag{2.29}$$

Solution. We write that X is $\mathrm{N}(\mu, \sigma^2)$. Then rv $Y = (X - \mu)/\sigma$ is $\mathrm{N}(0, 1)$, and

$$f_Y(y) = \frac{1}{\sqrt{(2\pi)}} \exp(-\tfrac{1}{2}y^2) \quad (-\infty < y < \infty)$$

Then we can show that

$$\phi_Y(\theta) = e^{-\frac{1}{2}\theta^2}$$

Therefore

$$\phi_X(\theta) = e^{i\theta\mu}\phi_Y(\theta\sigma) = e^{i\theta\mu}e^{-\frac{1}{2}(\theta\sigma)^2} = \exp(i\theta\mu - \tfrac{1}{2}\theta^2\sigma^2)$$ □

EXERCISES

1. If rv X is the value shown by a fair die, find EX, VX and pgf $G(s)$.

2. Deduce formula 2.15 from formula 2.9.

3. If X and Y are Bernoulli rvs, show that $Z = XY$ is also Bernoulli. If $X_1, \ldots, X_n$ are Bernoulli rvs, show that $Z_n = X_1 X_2 \ldots X_n$ is also Bernoulli.

4. Given

$$f_{Y|X=x}(y) = \begin{cases} 2y/x^2 & (0 < y < x) \\ 0 & \text{(otherwise)} \end{cases}$$

$$f_X(x) = \begin{cases} 4x^3 & (0 < x < 1) \\ 0 & \text{(otherwise)} \end{cases}$$

show that

(i) $$f_{X,Y}(x, y) = \begin{cases} 8xy & (0 < y < x < 1) \\ 0 & \text{(otherwise)} \end{cases}$$

(ii) $$f_Y(y) = \begin{cases} 4y(1-y^2) & (0 < y < 1) \\ 0 & \text{(otherwise)} \end{cases}$$

(iii) $$f_{X|Y=y}(x) = \begin{cases} 2x/(1-y^2) & (y < x < 1) \\ 0 & \text{(otherwise)} \end{cases}$$

(iv) $$\mathrm{pr}_{X,Y}(X > 2Y) = \tfrac{1}{4}$$

Note that in (iv),

$$\mathrm{pr}_{X,Y}(X > 2Y) = \iint\limits_{\{x,y:x>2y\}} f_{X,Y}(x, y)\,dxdy$$

5. If rv X has distribution $\mathrm{pr}_X(X = 1) = \tfrac{3}{4}$, $\mathrm{pr}_X(X = \tfrac{1}{5}) = \tfrac{1}{4}$, what is the distribution of rv $Z = 1/X$? What is the joint distribution of X and Z? Show that $\mathrm{cov}(X, Z) = -\tfrac{3}{5}$.

6. Prove formula 2.19 when X and Y are both continuous, and when X is discrete and Y is continuous.

7. If rv X has pgf $G(s)$, verify that $VX = G''(1) + G'(1) - \{G'(1)\}^2$.

8. If rv X is $\mathscr{P}(\lambda)$, show that $EX = VX = \lambda$.

9. If rv X is $\mathrm{Bin}(n, \theta)$, show that $EX = n\theta$, $VX = n\theta(1 - \theta)$.

17

10. The rv Y which is the number of independent Bernoulli trials (probability of success θ) up to but excluding the first success has a *geometric distribution* with parameter θ. We write Y is $\mathscr{G}(\theta)$, and

$$\text{pr}(Y = y) = (1-\theta)^y\theta \quad (y = 0, 1, 2, \ldots)$$

Show that Y has pgf $G(s) = \theta/\{1-(1-\theta)s\}$ and that $EY = (1-\theta)/\theta$, $VY = (1-\theta)/\theta^2$.

11. The rv W which is the number of failures in a sequence of independent Bernoulli trials (probability of success θ) prior to the nth success has a *negative binomial distribution* with parameters n and θ. We write W is $\text{NB}(n, \theta)$, and

$$\text{pr}(W = w) = \binom{n+w-1}{w}\theta^n(1-\theta)^w \quad (w = 0, 1, 2, \ldots)$$

Suppose that $Y_1, Y_2, \ldots, Y_n$ are independent $\mathscr{G}(\theta)$ rvs. By writing

$$W = Y_1 + Y_2 + \ldots + Y_n$$

deduce that W has pgf $G(s) = [\theta/\{1-(1-\theta)s\}]^n$, and that

$$EW = n(1-\theta)/\theta, \qquad VW = n(1-\theta)/\theta^2$$

12. If rv X is $\mathscr{P}(\lambda)$, and if the conditional distribution of Y given that $X = x$ is $\text{Bin}(x, \theta)$, show that the marginal distribution of Y is $\mathscr{P}(\lambda\theta)$. (Use Problem 2.14.)

13. Show that $V(aX+bY) = a^2VX + b^2VY + 2ab\,\text{cov}(X, Y)$.

14. If rv X is $\mathscr{E}(\lambda)$, show that its cf $\phi(\theta)$ is $\lambda/(\lambda-i\theta)$.

15. An rv Y having density

$$f_Y(y) = \begin{cases} \dfrac{\lambda}{\Gamma(\alpha)}(\lambda y)^{\alpha-1}e^{-\lambda y} & (y \geqslant 0) \\ 0 & (y < 0) \end{cases}$$

where $\Gamma(\alpha) = \int_0^\infty u^{\alpha-1}e^{-u}\,du$, has the *gamma* $(\alpha; \lambda)$ distribution. Show that Y has cf $\{\lambda/(\lambda-i\theta)\}^\alpha$. An $\mathscr{E}(\lambda)$ rv therefore has a gamma $(1; \lambda)$ distribution. Show that $EY = \alpha\lambda$, $VY = \alpha\lambda^2$.

16. If $X_1, \ldots, X_n$ are independent rvs, where X_k is gamma$(\alpha_k; \lambda)$, show that $Z_n = X_1 + \ldots + X_n$ is gamma $\left(\sum\limits_{k=1}^{n}\alpha_k; \lambda\right)$.

Chapter 3
The Random Walk

3.1 The unrestricted random walk

Problem 3.1 Consider the stochastic process which is the path of a particle which moves along an axis with steps of one unit at time intervals also of one unit. Suppose that the probability is p of any step being taken to the right, and is $q = 1 - p$ of being to the left. Suppose also that each step is taken independently of every other step. Then this process is called the *unrestricted random walk*. If the particle is in position 0 at time 0, determine the probability that it will be in position k after n steps.

Solution. Let $\{Z_n\}$ be the stochastic process, where Z_n is the position of the particle at time n, that is, after n steps from its starting point, 0. This stochastic process has a discrete time parameter space $\{0, 1, 2, \ldots\}$ and a discrete state space $\{-\infty, \ldots, -1, 0, 1, \ldots, \infty\}$. Now each step X is an independent rv having distribution

$$\operatorname{pr}(X = 1) = p, \qquad \operatorname{pr}(X = -1) = q$$

Initially $Z_0 = 0$. After n steps

$$Z_n = X_1 + X_2 + \ldots + X_n \tag{3.1}$$

where each X_i is independently distributed as X. We can write equation 3.1 as

$$Z_n = Z_{n-1} + X_n \tag{3.2}$$

where X_n is independent of Z_{n-1}.

We wish to determine the value of

$$p_{0k}^{(n)} = \operatorname{pr}(Z_n = k \mid Z_0 = 0) \tag{3.3}$$

Let rv

$$Y_i = \begin{cases} 1 & \text{if } X_i = 1 \\ 0 & \text{if } X_i = -1 \end{cases} \qquad (i = 1, 2, \ldots, n)$$

That is, let rv $Y_i = \frac{1}{2}(X_i + 1)$; then each Y_i is an independent Bernoulli trial with probability of success p. Then rv $R_n = Y_1 + \ldots + Y_n = \frac{1}{2}(Z_n + n)$ is $\operatorname{Bin}(n, p)$. Therefore, by equation 2.26

$$p_{0k}^{(n)} = \operatorname{pr}(Z_n = k \mid Z_0 = 0) = \operatorname{pr}\{R_n = \tfrac{1}{2}(Z_n + n) = \tfrac{1}{2}(k + n)\}$$

$$= \begin{cases} \dbinom{n}{\frac{1}{2}(k+n)} p^{\frac{1}{2}(k+n)} q^{\frac{1}{2}(n-k)} & (\tfrac{1}{2}(k+n) \in S = \{0, 1, 2, \ldots, n\}) \\ 0 & \text{(otherwise)}. \end{cases}$$

Since $ER_n = np$, $VR_n = npq$,

19

$$EZ_n = E(2R_n - n) = 2ER_n - n = n(p-q) \quad \text{(since } p+q = 1)$$
$$VZ_n = V(2R_n - n) = 4VR_n = 4npq \qquad \qquad \Box \quad (3.4)$$

We can call upon some quite deep theorems of probability theory to obtain the behaviour of Z_n when n is large. For example, by the *strong law of large numbers*, with probability one

$$\frac{1}{n}Z_n \to \frac{1}{n}EZ_n = p-q \quad \text{as} \quad n \to \infty$$

That is, for large n, the particle will, if $p > q$, almost certainly drift in a positive direction along the axis of motion, the mean step length being $p-q$. Also, by the *central limit theorem*,

$$W_n = \frac{Z_n - n(p-q)}{\sqrt{(4npq)}} \to \text{an N}(0,1) \text{ rv as } n \to \infty$$

So, from tables of the N$(0,1)$ distribution, for large n,

$$\text{pr}(-1\cdot96 < W_n \leqslant 1\cdot96) \approx 0\cdot95$$

i.e. $\text{pr}\{n(p-q) - 1\cdot96\sqrt{(4npq)} < Z_n \leqslant n(p-q) + 1\cdot96\sqrt{(4npq)}\} \approx 0\cdot95$.

Problem 3.2 Find approximate 95% bounds for $Z_{10\,000}$ if $p = 0\cdot6$.

Solution. $q = 0\cdot4$

Therefore, $EZ = 10\,000(0\cdot6 - 0\cdot4) = 2000$

$\sqrt{VZ} = \sqrt{(4 \times 10\,000 \times 0\cdot6 \times 0\cdot4)} = \sqrt{9600} = 40\sqrt{6} \approx 98$

Therefore, $\qquad\qquad 1\cdot96\sqrt{VZ} \approx 1\cdot96 \times 98 \approx 192$

Therefore $\text{pr}(2000 - 192 < Z_{10\,000} \leqslant 2000 + 192) \approx 0\cdot95$

i.e. $\qquad\qquad\qquad \text{pr}(1808 < Z_{10\,000} \leqslant 2192) \approx 0\cdot95$

A superficial acquaintance with the theory of statistics is sufficient to tell us that with $n = 10\,000$ the approximation will be very good indeed. $\quad\Box$

Problem 3.3 Find approximate 95% bounds for $Z_{10\,000}$ if $p = 0\cdot5$.

Solution. $EZ = 0$. $\sqrt{VZ} = \sqrt{(4 \times 10\,000 \times 0\cdot5 \times 0\cdot5)} = 100$. Therefore,

$$\text{pr}(-200 < Z_{10\,000} \leqslant 200) \approx 0\cdot95 \qquad\qquad \Box$$

Now $\sqrt{VZ}$ is maximum when $p = \frac{1}{2}$. Therefore after 10 000 steps, which would allow the particle to be up to 10 000 steps on either side of its starting point, it is, with 95% certainty, effectively restricted to within ± 200 steps.

Problem 3.4 Evaluate the generating function

$$P_{0k}(s) = \sum_{n=0}^{\infty} p_{0k}^{(n)} s^n$$

for $k = 0$ and $k = 1$, where $p_{0k}^{(n)}$ is defined in equation 3.3.

Solution. These are *not* pgfs, since $p_{0k}^{(n)}$ $(n = 0, 1, 2, \ldots)$ is not a probability distribution, it being possible for the particle to be in position k for many different values of n on the same random walk. For example, $p_{00}^{(0)} = 1$,

$$p_{00}^{(2)} = \binom{2}{1} pq = 2pq, \text{ so } \sum_n p_{00}^{(n)} \geq 1 + 2pq > 1.$$

$$P_{00}(s) = \sum_{n = 0, 2, 4, \ldots} \binom{n}{\frac{1}{2}n} p^{\frac{1}{2}n} q^{\frac{1}{2}n} s^n = \sum_{m = \frac{1}{2}n = 0}^{\infty} \binom{2m}{m} (pqs^2)^m$$

$$= (1 - 4pqs^2)^{-\frac{1}{2}} = u(s), \quad \text{say} \qquad (3.5)$$

(We might recognise this as the *Legendre polynomial generating function*.)

Now

$$\binom{2n+1}{n} = \frac{(2n+1)!}{(n+1)! \, n!} = \frac{2(n+1) - 1}{n+1} \cdot \frac{(2n)!}{n! \, n!} = \left(2 - \frac{1}{n+1}\right) \binom{2n}{n} \qquad (3.6)$$

and

$$\sum_{n=0}^{\infty} \binom{2n}{n} \frac{w^{n+1}}{n+1} = \sum_{n=0}^{\infty} \binom{2n}{n} \int_0^w x^n \, dx = \int_0^w \left\{ \sum_{n=0}^{\infty} \binom{2n}{n} x^n \right\} dx$$

$$= \int_0^w \frac{dx}{\sqrt{(1 - 4x)}} \qquad \text{(by comparison with equation 3.5)}$$

$$= \tfrac{1}{2}\{1 - \sqrt{(1 - 4w)}\} \qquad (3.7)$$

Therefore

$$P_{01}(s) = \sum_{n=0}^{\infty} p_{01}^{(2n+1)} s^{2n+1} = \sum_{n=0}^{\infty} \binom{2n+1}{n} p^{n+1} q^n s^{2n+1}$$

$$= 2ps \sum_{n=0}^{\infty} \binom{2n}{n} (pqs^2)^n - \frac{1}{qs} \sum_{n=0}^{\infty} \binom{2n}{n} \frac{(pqs^2)^{n+1}}{n+1} \qquad \text{(by equation 3.6)}$$

$$= 2ps(1 - 4pqs^2)^{-\frac{1}{2}} - \frac{1}{2qs}\{1 - (1 - 4pqs^2)^{\frac{1}{2}}\} = \frac{1}{2qs}\{u(s) - 1\}$$

(by equations 3.5 and 3.7) $\qquad \square$

We shall in future try to find solutions which are based on probability arguments rather than analytical techniques.

In Section 4.4 we shall meet a formula by which, from $P_{00}(s)$ and $P_{01}(s)$ we can calculate $P_{0k}(s)$ for any integer k.

3.2 Types of stochastic process A process $\{Z_t : t \in T \subseteq (-\infty, \infty)\}$ such that for any $\{t_1, t_2, \ldots, t_n\} \in T$, where $t_1 < t_2 < \ldots < t_n$, the rvs

$$Z_{t_2} - Z_{t_1}, Z_{t_3} - Z_{t_2}, \ldots, Z_{t_n} - Z_{t_{n-1}}$$

are independent, is called a *process with independent increments*.

A stochastic process $\{Z_t : t \in T \equiv (-\infty, \infty)\}$ is *stationary* if, for any $\{t_1, t_2, \ldots, t_n\} \in T$ the joint probability distributions of

$$Z_{t_1 + \tau}, Z_{t_2 + \tau}, \ldots, Z_{t_n + \tau}$$

and

$$Z_{t_1}, Z_{t_2}, \ldots, Z_{t_n}$$

are the same for all $\tau \in (-\infty, \infty)$; and is *stationary in the wide sense* if the *covariance function* $g(t, t + \tau) = \text{cov}(Z_t, Z_{t+\tau}) = g(\tau)$, is a function of τ only, for all $t \in T$.

A process with independent increments has $g(t, t + \tau) = g(t) \, (\tau > 0)$.

A *Markov process* is a stochastic process $\{Z_t : t \in T \subseteq (-\infty, \infty)\}$ for which, given the value of Z_t the distribution of $Z_s \, (s > t)$ in no way depends on a knowledge of $Z_u \, (u < t)$. The future behaviour, when the present state of the process is known, is unchanged by additional knowledge about its past behaviour. Thus if

$$\tau_0 < \tau_1 < \ldots < \tau_k < t_1 < t_2 < \ldots < t_n$$

then the joint distributions of

$$Z_{t_1}, \ldots, Z_{t_n} \mid Z_{\tau_0} = z_0, \ldots, Z_{\tau_k} = z_k$$

and of

$$Z_{t_1}, \ldots, Z_{t_n} \mid Z_{\tau_k} = z_k$$

are the same. This is referred to as the *Markov property*.

Markov processes are by far the most important class of stochastic processes and their theory is highly developed. Every stochastic process with independent increments is a Markov process.

Problem 3.5 Show that the unrestricted random walk is a stochastic process with independent increments (and so is also Markov), and is stationary under translations by integer intervals.

Solution. If $\{X_k\}$ is a sequence of independent rvs, then $\{Z_n\}$, where $Z_n = \sum_{k=1}^{n} X_k$, has independent increments since if $n_0 < n_1 < n_2$ then

$$Z_{n_1} - Z_{n_0} = \sum_{k=n_0+1}^{n_1} X_k \text{ and } Z_{n_2} - Z_{n_1} = \sum_{k=n_1+1}^{n_2} X_k \text{ are independent.}$$

The position of the particle at time n is Z_n and since the probabilities of stepping to the right or left in no way depend on Z_n the joint distribution of $Z_{n_0}, Z_{n_1}, \ldots, Z_{n_k}$ depends only on the time intervals between the observations, and so is the same as the joint distribution of $Z_{n_0+m}, Z_{n_1+m}, \ldots, Z_{n_k+m}$ for all $m \in (\ldots, -1, 0, 1, 2, \ldots)$. $\square$

3.3 The gambler's ruin

Problem 3.6 *The random walk with two absorbing barriers.* Two adversaries, A and B, have resources £a and £b respectively. They play a game in which each play results in A winning £1 from B with probability p, or B winning £1 from A with probability $q = 1 - p$. Each play is independent of every other play. Find the probability that A will eventually have to withdraw on losing his entire £a.

Solution. Define rv

$$Y = \begin{cases} 1 & \text{if } A \text{ is eventually ruined} \\ 0 & \text{otherwise} \end{cases}$$

Then rv Y has a Bernoulli distribution with, as its probability of success, the probability that A is eventually ruined. We consider the random-walk process $\{Z_n : n = 0, 1, 2, \ldots\}$, where $Z_n + a$ are the resources (in £) of A after the nth play. Then $Z_0 = 0$ and the state space

$$S = \{-a, -a+1, \ldots, -1, 0, 1, 2, \ldots, b-1, b\}$$

The game will cease when A has won B's £b, or when B has won A's £a, i.e. when Z_n first reaches $-a$ or b; thereafter Z_{n+1}, Z_{n+2}, $\ldots$ will all take the same value as Z_n. These states $-a$ and b are called *absorbing states*.

Rv $Y = 1$ if Z_n reaches $-a$ before it reaches b, and $Y = 0$ otherwise. We seek $\mathrm{pr}(Y = 1 \mid Z_0 = 0)$.

Let us write

$$G_i(s) = \mathrm{E}_{Y\mid Z_0 = i} s^Y = 1 - \theta_i + \theta_i s = 1 - (1-s)\theta_i \quad (i \in S)$$

the pgf for the Bernoulli rv Y given that the walk starts in state i, where $\theta_i = \mathrm{pr}(Y = 1 \mid Z_0 = i)$.

We find a set of recurrence relations for the G_i, which we solve for θ_0. Clearly $\theta_{-a} = 1$, $\theta_b = 0$.

We need some preliminary results. Clearly

$$\mathrm{pr}(Y = 1 \mid Z_n = i) = \theta_i$$

irrespective of n. Also, since the plays are independent, the random walk has the Markov property, so

$$\mathrm{E}_{Y\mid Z_1 = k, Z_0 = i} s^Y = \mathrm{E}_{Y\mid Z_1 = k} s^Y = G_k(s) \quad (i, k \in S)$$

Then, by the decomposition rule,

$$G_i(s) = \mathrm{E}_{Y\mid Z_0 = i} s^Y = \mathrm{E}_{Y, Z_1 \mid Z_0 = i} s^Y = \mathrm{E}_{Z_1 \mid Z_0 = i} \mathrm{E}_{Y\mid Z_1 = Z_1, Z_0 = i} s^Y$$
$$= \mathrm{E}_{Z_1 \mid Z_0 = i} G_{Z_1}(s)$$

Therefore

$$1 - \theta_i = G_i(0) = \mathrm{E}_{Z_1 \mid Z_0 = i} G_{Z_1}(0) = \mathrm{E}_{Z_1 \mid Z_0 = i}(1 - \theta_{Z_1}) = 1 - \mathrm{E}_{Z_1 \mid Z_0 = i} \theta_{Z_1}$$

so

$$\theta_i = E_{Z_1|Z_0=i}\theta_{Z_1}$$
$$= \theta_{i-1}\mathrm{pr}(Z_1 = i-1\,|\,Z_0 = i) + \theta_{i+1}\,\mathrm{pr}(Z_1 = i+1\,|\,Z_0 = i)$$
$$= q\theta_{i-1} + p\theta_{i+1} \quad (i = -a+1,\ldots,b-1). \tag{3.8}$$

This is a sequence of $a+b-2$ second-order difference equations in $a+b-2$ unknowns. These equations can generally be written down directly with just a brief explanation. The use of generating functions introduces an extra flexibility in allowing us to abstract from our results any of those aspects of the process which interest us. In this problem there is a one–one correspondence between G_i and θ_i, so this is unnecessary. The decomposition rule applied in this way is sometimes referred to as a *decomposition based on the first step*. We now solve the equations for θ_0. We write equation 3.8 in the form

$$(p+q)\theta_i = q\theta_{i-1} + p\theta_{i+1}$$

so

$$p(\theta_{i+1} - \theta_i) = q(\theta_i - \theta_{i-1}) \quad (i = -a+1,\ldots,b-1)$$

Write $I_i = \theta_i - \theta_{i-1}$, and $\lambda = q/p$. Then

$$I_i = \lambda I_{i-1} = \lambda(\lambda I_{i-2}) = \ldots = \lambda^i I_0$$

Then

$$-1 = \theta_b - \theta_{-a} = \sum_{i=-a+1}^{b} (\theta_i - \theta_{i-1}) = \sum_{i=-a+1}^{b} I_i = I_0 \sum_{i=-a+1}^{b} \lambda^i,$$

and similarly, by writing $a = 0$,

$$-\theta_0 = \theta_b - \theta_0 = I_0 \sum_{i=1}^{b} \lambda^i$$

so

$$\theta_0 = \sum_{i=1}^{b} \lambda^i \Big/ \sum_{i=-a+1}^{b} \lambda^i = \begin{cases} \dfrac{b}{a+b} & (\lambda = 1, \text{ i.e. } p = q = \tfrac{1}{2}) \\[2ex] \dfrac{\lambda^b - 1}{\lambda^b - \lambda^{-a}} & (\lambda = q/p \neq 1) \end{cases} \qquad \square \tag{3.9}$$

Problem 3.7   What is the probability that A is eventually triumphant?

Solution. Let rv

$$Y^* = \begin{cases} 1 \text{ if } A \text{ is eventually triumphant} \\ 0 \text{ otherwise} \end{cases}$$

and let

$$\phi_i = \mathrm{pr}(Y^* = 1\,|\,Z_0 = i)$$
$$= \mathrm{pr}\{A \text{ is eventually triumphant}\,|\,A \text{ starts with } \pounds(a+i)\}$$

24

$$= \text{pr}\{B \text{ is eventually ruined} \mid B \text{ starts with } £(b-i)\}$$

Then we would obtain the same equations as in Problem 3.6, but with a and b interchanged, p and q interchanged, and i changed to $-i$. Thus, from equation 3.9,

$$\phi_0 = \begin{cases} \dfrac{a}{a+b} & (\lambda = 1, \quad \text{i.e. } p = q = \tfrac{1}{2}) \\[2ex] \dfrac{1-\lambda^a}{1-\lambda^{a+b}} & (\lambda = q/p \neq 1) \end{cases} \qquad \square$$

Problem 3.8 Show that it is certain that the game eventually ends.

Solution. The probability that the game eventually ends is the probability that A is either eventually ruined or triumphant

$$= \text{pr}(Y = 1 \mid Z_0 = 0) + \text{pr}(Y^* = 1 \mid Z_0 = 0)$$
$$= \theta_0 + \phi_0 = 1 \quad (\text{all } p, q > 0 \text{ for which } p+q = 1)$$

Thus with probability 1, the game will eventually end. That is, for the random walk with two absorbing barriers, absorption is certain with probability 1. $\qquad \square$

Problem 3.9 Find the distribution of the duration, T, of the game.

Solution. Let

$$F_i(s) = \text{E}_{T \mid Z_0 = i} s^T = \sum_{n=0}^{\infty} f_i^{(n)} s^n$$

where

$$f_i^{(n)} = \text{pr}(T = n \mid Z_0 = i) = \text{pr}\{\text{game ends on } n\text{th play} \mid A \text{ starts}$$
$$\text{with } £(a+i)\}$$

Given $Z_1 = j$, then by the Markov property and time independence

$$T = 1 + T'$$

where T' has pgf $F_j(s)$
i.e.
$$\text{E}_{T \mid Z_1 = j, Z_0 = i} s^T = \text{E}_{T' \mid Z_0 = j} s^{1+T'} = s F_j(s)$$

Then, by a decomposition based on the first step,

$$F_i(s) = \text{E}_{T, Z_1 \mid Z_0 = i} s^T = \text{E}_{Z_1 \mid Z_0 = i} \text{E}_{T \mid Z_1 = Z_1, Z_0 = i} s^T$$
$$= s \text{E}_{Z_1 \mid Z_0 = i} F_{Z_1}(s) = s\{q F_{i-1}(s) + p F_{i+1}(s)\} \quad (i = -a+1, \ldots, b-1)$$

We have the boundary conditions that

$$F_{-a}(s) = \text{E}_{T \mid Z_0 = -a} s^T = \text{E}s^0 = 1$$

and $F_b(s) = 1$ similarly. We seek $F_0(s)$. The general solution is

$$F_i(s) = A(s)\{\alpha(s)\}^i + B(s)\{\beta(s)\}^i$$

25

where $\alpha(s)$ and $\beta(s)$ are the roots $\{1 \mp \sqrt{(1-4pqs^2)}\}/2ps$ of the quadratic equation

$$v = s(q + pv^2) \tag{3.10}$$

and $A(s)$ and $B(s)$ are determined from the boundary conditions. Then

$$F_{-a}(s) = 1 = A\alpha^{-a} + B\beta^{-a}$$
$$F_b(s) = 1 = A\alpha^b + B\beta^b$$

have solution

$$A = \frac{\beta^b - \beta^{-a}}{\alpha^{-a}\beta^b - \alpha^b\beta^{-a}}, \qquad B = -\frac{\alpha^b - \alpha^{-a}}{\alpha^{-a}\beta^b - \alpha^b\beta^{-a}}$$

Then $F_0(s) = A + B$. $\qquad\qquad\qquad\qquad\qquad\qquad\qquad\qquad\square$

When $s = 1$, $\alpha(1) = 1$ and $\beta(1) = \lambda = q/p$; and for $\lambda \neq 1$ we find $F_0(1) = 1$. When $\lambda = 1$ we can set $\beta = \alpha(1+\varepsilon)$ in the solution and let $\varepsilon \to 0$. Since

$$F_0(1) = \sum_{n=0}^{\infty} f_0^{(n)} = 1$$

$$\mathrm{pr}(T \geqslant k \,|\, Z_0 = 0) = \sum_{n=k}^{\infty} f_0^{(n)} \to 0 \quad \text{as} \quad k \to \infty$$

With probability 1, therefore, the game eventually ends. This is another solution to Problem 3.8.

Problem 3.10 *The random walk with a single absorbing barrier.* What is the probability of A's eventual ruin if he is playing against a casino which has unlimited capital?

Solution. If we let the casino be adversary B, and have unlimited resources, then the probability of A's eventual ruin, given that he begins with £a, is

$$\lim_{b \to \infty} \theta_0 = \begin{cases} \displaystyle\lim_{b \to \infty} \frac{1}{\dfrac{a}{b}+1} & (p = q = \tfrac{1}{2}) \\[2ex] \displaystyle\lim_{b \to \infty} \frac{1 - \lambda^{-b}}{1 - \lambda^{-a}\lambda^{-b}} & (\lambda = q/p > 1) \\[2ex] \displaystyle\lim_{b \to \infty} \frac{\lambda^b - 1}{\lambda^b - \lambda^{-a}} & (\lambda = q/p < 1) \end{cases}$$

$$= \begin{cases} 1 & (p \leqslant q) \\[1ex] \left(\dfrac{q}{p}\right)^a & (p > q) \end{cases}$$

since $\lambda^{-b} \to 0$ if $\lambda > 1$, and $\lambda^b \to 0$ if $\lambda < 1$. Hence, if $p > q$, there is a probability $(q/p)^a$ that gambler A is eventually ruined, but there is probability $1 - (q/p)^a$ that the game never ends. We say that the random walk has *positive drift* if $p > q$. On the other hand, if $p \leqslant q$ (that is, if there is *zero* or *negative drift*) gambler A will almost certainly be ruined, i.e. with probability 1 he will reach the barrier at $-a$. $\qquad \Box$

Thus if $p \leqslant q$, as it always will be in any casino, the gambler knows that eventually he will be ruined. However, what will be of interest to him is the distribution of the time before he loses all his money. We investigate this *time to absorption* in the next problem.

Problem 3.11 *The time to absorption.* Find the probability distribution of the rv T_{a0}, the number of plays made before a gambler who starts with £a is ruined, given that $p \leqslant q$.

Solution. For convenience we now take our single absorbing barrier to be state 0 (not state $-a$ as before), and consider the stochastic process $\{Z_n : n = 0, 1, 2, \ldots\}$, where Z_n is the capital of the gambler after the nth play. Then $Z_0 = a$. Now

$$F_{a0}(s) = \mathrm{E}_{T|Z_0 = a} s^T = \mathrm{E}s^{T_{a0}} = \lim_{b \to \infty} F_0(s)$$

where $F_0(s)$ is the solution of Problem 3.9. Suppose $p < q$, then, from equation 3.10, $\alpha(s)\beta(s) = q/p > 1$. Therefore $|\beta(s)| > 1$, so $\{\beta(s)\}^b$ is unbounded as $b \to \infty$. Therefore, since $F_b(s)$ is bounded as $b \to \infty$, $B(s) = 0$. Then

$$F_{00}(s) = \lim_{b \to \infty} F_{-a}(s) = 1 = A(s)\{\alpha(s)\}^{-a}$$

so

$$F_{a0}(s) = \lim_{b \to \infty} F_0(s) = A(s) = \{\alpha(s)\}^a = \left\{ \frac{1 - \sqrt{(1 - 4pqs^2)}}{2ps} \right\}^a$$

This also holds when $p = q = \frac{1}{2}$. $\qquad \Box$

Alternatively we note that for £a to be reduced to £0 *for the first time*, it must be reduced successively *for the first time* to £$(a-1)$, to £$(a-2)$, and so on to £1 and finally to £0. During each of these unit reductions the gambler's capital can rise, but eventually, since $p \leqslant q$, it will fall. Let rv T_{ij} $(j < i)$ be the number of plays for the gambler's capital to be reduced for the first time from £i to £j. Then

$$T_{a0} = T_{a, a-1} + T_{a-1, a-2} + \ldots + T_{10} \qquad (3.11)$$

But the time taken to lose a pound does not depend on which pound it is, so by this time independence each $T_{k, k-1}$ is distributed as T_{10}, and these $T_{k, k-1}$ are mutually independent by the Markov property. Thus

27

c

$$F_{a0}(s) = \{F_{10}(s)\}^a$$

We need therefore determine only $F_{10}(s)$. We find an alternative derivation of this in Problem 4.18.

Problem 3.12 *The random walk with a single reflecting barrier.* Consider a random walk such that the particle, when it reaches state 0, moves on the next step to state 1 with probability 1, and resumes its random walk behaviour (Figure 3.1). Then state 0 is called a *reflecting barrier*.

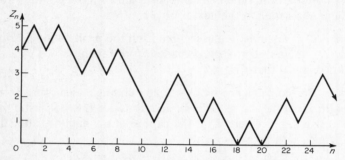

Figure 3.1 The random walk with a single reflecting barrier

If this random walk process $\{Z_n : n = 0, 1, 2, \ldots\}$ starts in state i ($i \in S = \{0, 1, 2, \ldots\}$), determine a set of difference equations for the pgf $\Pi_i^{(n)}(s)$ for the position of the particle at time n.

Solution. We consider a decomposition based on the *last* step.

$$\Pi_i^{(n+1)}(s) = \mathrm{E}_{Z_{n+1}|Z_0=i}\, s^{Z_{n+1}} = \mathrm{E}_{Z_n|Z_0=i}\{\mathrm{E}_{Z_{n+1}|Z_n=Z_n,Z_0=i}\, s^{Z_{n+1}}\}$$

Now

$$Z_{n+1} = \begin{cases} Z_n+1 & \text{with probability } p \quad (Z_n \neq 0) \\ Z_n-1 & \text{with probability } q \quad (Z_n \neq 0) \\ 1 & (Z_n = 0) \end{cases}$$

so, by the Markov property,

$$\mathrm{E}_{Z_{n+1}|Z_n=Z_n,Z_0=i}\, s^{Z_{n+1}} = \mathrm{E}_{Z_{n+1}|Z_n=Z_n}\, s^{Z_{n+1}}$$
$$= \begin{cases} ps^{Z_n+1}+qs^{Z_n-1} = (ps+qs^{-1})s^{Z_n} & (Z_n \neq 0) \\ s = (ps+qs^{-1})s^{Z_n}+q(s-s^{-1}) & (Z_n = 0) \end{cases}$$

Therefore

$$\Pi_i^{(n+1)}(s) = q(s-s^{-1})\mathrm{pr}(Z_n = 0 \mid Z_0 = i)+\mathrm{E}_{Z_n|Z_0=i}(ps+qs^{-1})s^{Z_n}$$
$$= q(s-s^{-1})\Pi_i^{(n)}(0)+(ps+qs^{-1})\Pi_i^{(n)}(s) \tag{3.12}$$

The initial condition is $\Pi_i^{(0)}(s) = \mathrm{E}_{Z_0|Z_0=i}\, s^{Z_0} = s^i$. $\qquad\square$

28

Problem 3.13   On the random walk of Problem 3.12, if $p \leqslant q$, the particle is certain to return to state 0 from any positive state i (by Problem 3.10). It will therefore spend periods away from the reflecting barrier broken up by single steps onto it. By the Markov property, after first stepping onto the barrier, the process is in a statistical equilibrium, independent of the initial starting state, and the periods off the barrier are independent and identically distributed random variables. Find the equilibrium distribution of Z_n as $n \to \infty$, and show that this solution exists only if p is strictly less than q.

Solution. Let $\Pi_i^{(n)}(s) \to \Pi(s) = \sum\limits_{j=0}^{\infty} \pi_j s^j$ as $n \to \infty$. Then, letting $n \to \infty$ in equation 3.12,

$$\Pi(s) = (s - s^{-1})q\,\Pi(0) + (ps + qs^{-1})\Pi(s)$$

i.e.

$$\Pi(s) = \frac{(s - s^{-1})q\pi_0}{1 - (ps + qs^{-1})} = \frac{(1+s)\pi_0}{1 - vs}, \quad \text{where } v = p/q$$

Now $\Pi(1) = 1$. Therefore, $1 = 2\pi_0/(1-v)$, so $\Pi(0) = \pi_0 = \frac{1}{2}(1-v) = 1 - 1/(2q)$.

We note that if $v = p/q = 1$ then $\pi_0 = 0$; and so $\Pi(s) = 0$, which is not a pgf. Similarly if $v > 1$, i.e. $p > q$, then $\pi_0 < 0$, so π_0 is not even a probability. If $v < 1$ then

$$\Pi(s) = \frac{(1-v)(1+s)}{2(1-vs)} = \frac{1}{2}(1-v) + \frac{1}{2}(1+v)\frac{(1-v)s}{1-vs}$$

$$= \pi_0 \Pi_U(s) + (1 - \pi_0)\Pi_W(s)$$

where $\Pi_U(s) = 1$ is the pgf of an rv U which is 0 with probability 1, and $\Pi_W(s) = (1-v)s/(1-vs) = s\,\Pi_V(s)$ is the pgf of an rv $W = V + 1$, where V has a geometric distribution with parameter $1 - v = 2 - q^{-1}$. The rv U corresponds to the time on the barrier and W to the time off it. $\square$

The form of $\Pi(s)$ is that of a *mixture* of the pgfs of the two rvs U and W. A mixture is the result of a two-stage experiment. First we decide according to the result of a Bernoulli trial with probability of success π_0 whether to observe rv U or rv W. If a success results then we observe U, otherwise W. This model has the same probability behaviour as the equilibrium distribution of the random walk.

We shall be meeting a theory for equilibrium distributions later.

Problem 3.14   Consider a random walk on $(0, 1, 2, \ldots, a)$, where at each step $p = q = \frac{1}{2}$. State 0 is absorbing, and state a is *impenetrable* with $\mathrm{pr}(Z_{n+1} = a \mid Z_n = a) = \frac{1}{2}$, $\mathrm{pr}(Z_{n+1} = a-1 \mid Z_n = a) = \frac{1}{2}$. (That is, if the particle is in an *impenetrable* state, then at the next step with some fixed probability θ it remains in that state for a further time unit, otherwise with

29

probability $1 - \theta$ it retreats a step and resumes its random-walk behaviour.) Show that if the particle starts in state $i (\neq 0)$ then absorption is certain, and determine the expected time to absorption.

Solution. We consider a decomposition based on the first step. Let $F_k(s)$ be the pgf for the first passage time T_k from state k to state 0. Then, for $k = 1, 2, \ldots, a-1$,

$$F_k(s) = Es^{T_k} = Es^{1+T_{k-1}}\mathrm{pr}(Z_1 = k-1 | Z_0 = k)$$
$$+ Es^{1+T_{k+1}}\mathrm{pr}(Z_1 = k+1 | Z_0 = k)$$
$$= \tfrac{1}{2}s F_{k-1}(s) + \tfrac{1}{2}s F_{k+1}(s) \tag{3.13}$$

The boundary conditions are

$$F_0(s) = Es^{T_0} = Es^0 = 1 \tag{3.14}$$

and

$$F_a(s) = Es^{1+T_{a-1}}\mathrm{pr}(Z_1 = a-1 | Z_0 = a)$$
$$+ Es^{1+T_a}\mathrm{pr}(Z_1 = a | Z_0 = a)$$
$$= \tfrac{1}{2}s F_{a-1}(s) + \tfrac{1}{2}s F_a(s) \tag{3.15}$$

We consider the case $s = 1$, then solving equation 3.13 successively starting with the last equation (3.15) we find $F_k(1) = 1$ $(k = 0, 1, 2, \ldots, a)$, so absorption must take place with some finite n (with probability 1). (See Problem 3.9.)

Let

$$M_k = ET_k = \frac{d}{ds}\{F_k(s)\}\bigg|_{s=1}$$

then $M_k < \infty$ and, from equations 3.13, 3.14 and 3.15, satisfies

$$M_k = 1 + \tfrac{1}{2}M_{k-1} + \tfrac{1}{2}M_{k+1} \quad (k = 1, 2, \ldots, a-1)$$
$$M_0 = 0 \tag{3.16}$$
$$M_a = 1 + \tfrac{1}{2}M_{a-1} + \tfrac{1}{2}M_a$$

We note that these are solved by $M_0 = 0$, $M_k = \infty$ $(k = 1, 2, \ldots, a)$, but since absorption occurs with probability 1 within a finite time, we can rule out this solution. Let $I_k = M_k - M_{k-1}$ $(k = 1, 2, \ldots, a)$, then equations 3.16 reduce to

$$I_k = I_{k+1} + 2 \quad (k = 1, 2, \ldots, a-1), \qquad I_a = 2$$

so

$$I_k = 2(a+1-k) \quad (k = 1, 2, \ldots, a)$$

Therefore

$$M_i = M_i - M_0 = (M_i - M_{i-1}) + (M_{i-1} - M_{i-2}) + \ldots + (M_1 - M_0)$$
$$= \sum_{k=1}^{i} I_k = 2\sum_{k=1}^{i}(a+1-k) = i(2a+1-i). \qquad \square$$

Problem 3.15 A particle executes a random walk on the vertices of a cube. The steps are independent, and the particle always steps with equal probability to one of its three neighbouring vertices. If A and H are opposite vertices, find the pgf for the first passage time from A to H, i.e. the time at which a particle which sets out from A first reaches H.

If A and H are absorbing states, what is the probability of absorption at H given that the walk starts at a vertex which is neither A nor H?

Solution. Label the vertices of the cube as in Figure 3.2.

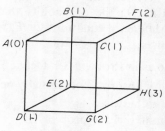

Figure 3.2

Define states for the system by the minimum number of steps from the vertices to A. Then if the particle is at A, it is in state 0; if at B, C or D it is in state 1; if at E, F or G it is in state 2; and if at H it is in state 3. Let T_i be the first passage time from state i to state 3 ($i = 0, 1, 2, 3$), then $T_3 = 0$. If $F_i(s) = Es^{T_i}$, we seek $F_0(s)$. We consider decompositions based on the first step X.

$$F_0(s) = Es^{T_0} = Es^{1+T_1} = sF_1(s)$$

since from state 0 the first step must be to state 1.

$$F_1(s) = E_X E_{T_1 | X = x} s^{T_1} = \tfrac{1}{3}Es^{1+T_0} + \tfrac{2}{3}Es^{1+T_2} = \tfrac{1}{3}sF_0(s) + \tfrac{2}{3}sF_2(s)$$

since, with probability $\tfrac{1}{3}$, the first step is to state 0 or, with probability $\tfrac{2}{3}$, to state 2. Similarly

$$F_2(s) = \tfrac{2}{3}sF_1(s) + \tfrac{1}{3}sF_3(s) = \tfrac{2}{3}sF_1(s) + \tfrac{1}{3}s$$

since $F_3(s) = Es^0 = 1$. We can solve these to obtain

$$F_0(s) = 2s^3/(9 - 7s^2) \quad (\text{so } ET_0 = 10)$$

Now suppose that states 0 and 3 are absorbing. Let $\theta_i (i = 0, 1, 2, 3)$ be the probability of absorption in state 3 if the particle starts in state i. We seek the values of θ_1 and θ_2. Clearly $\theta_0 = 0$, $\theta_3 = 1$. By decompositions based on the first step, starting in state 1 and state 2 respectively, we obtain

31

$$\theta_1 = \tfrac{1}{3}\theta_0 + \tfrac{2}{3}\theta_2, \qquad \theta_2 = \tfrac{2}{3}\theta_1 + \tfrac{1}{3}\theta_3$$

so
$$\theta_1 = \tfrac{2}{5}, \qquad \theta_2 = \tfrac{3}{5} \qquad\qquad \square$$

3.4 Generalisations of the random-walk model
Instead of just a single step at each time instant we can allow larger jumps.

Problem 3.16 Suppose that in a random walk the steps are independently distributed as a discrete rv X, where $\mathrm{pr}(X = k) = p_k$ ($k = \dots, -1, 0, 1, 2, \dots$); and that there are absorbing barriers at integers $-a$ and b ($a, b > 0$), the process being absorbed as soon as the walk reaches or passes over a barrier. Suppose that the process starts in state i. Find difference equations for θ_i, the probability that absorption eventually occurs at $-a$. Find difference equations for $F_i(s)$, the pgf for the time to absorption of the process.

Solution. We argue as in Problem 3.6. Define Bernoulli rv
$$Y = \begin{cases} 1 & \text{if absorption eventually occurs at } -a \\ 0 & \text{otherwise} \end{cases}$$
and consider the random walk process $\{Z_n : n = 0, 1, 2, \dots\}$, where Z_n is the position of the particle after n steps. We seek difference equations for $\theta_i = \mathrm{pr}(Y = 1 \mid Z_0 = i)$. We use a decomposition based on the first step:
$$\mathrm{pr}(Y = 1 \mid Z_0 = i)$$
$$= \sum_{j=-\infty}^{\infty} \mathrm{pr}(Z_1 = j \mid Z_0 = i)\mathrm{pr}(Y = 1 \mid Z_0 = i, Z_1 = j),$$
i.e.
$$\theta_i = \sum_{j=-\infty}^{\infty} p_{j-i}\theta_j \qquad (i \in I \equiv \{-a+1, -a+2, \dots, b-1\})$$
by the Markov property. Clearly
$$\theta_{-\infty} = \dots = \theta_{-a-1} = \theta_{-a} = 1, \qquad \theta_b = \theta_{b+1} = \dots = \theta_\infty = 0.$$
Therefore
$$\theta_i = 1 \times \sum_{j=-\infty}^{-a} p_{j-i} + \sum_{j=-a+1}^{b-1} p_{j-i}\theta_j + 0 \times \sum_{j=b}^{\infty} p_{j-i}$$
$$= g_i + \sum_{j \in I} p_{j-i}\theta_j \qquad (i \in I)$$
where
$$g_i = \sum_{k=j-i=-\infty}^{-a-i} p_k = \mathrm{pr}(X \leqslant -a-i)$$

As in Problem 3.9, if rv T is the time to absorption, then if $Z_0 = i$ ($i \in I$) and $Z_1 = j$ we can write $T = 1 + T'$, where, if $j \in I$, T' has pgf $F_j(s)$, but if $j \notin I$ then $T' = 0$; i.e.

32

$$\mathrm{E}_{T|Z_1=j,Z_0=i} s^T = \mathrm{E}_{T'|Z_0=j} s^{1+T'} = \begin{cases} sF_j(s) & (j \in I) \\ s & (j \notin I) \end{cases}$$

Therefore

$$F_i(s) = \mathrm{E}_{Z_1|Z_0=i}\, \mathrm{E}_{T|Z_1=Z_1,Z_0=i} s^T$$

$$= s\left\{ \sum_{j=-\infty}^{-a} p_{j-i} + \sum_{j=-a+1}^{b-1} p_{j-i} F_j(s) + \sum_{j=b}^{\infty} p_{j-i} \right\} \quad (i \in I)$$

$$= s\left\{ g_i^* + \sum_{j \in I} p_{j-i} F_j(s) \right\} \quad (i \in I)$$

where

$$g_i^* = \mathrm{pr}(X \leqslant -a-i \quad \text{or} \quad X \geqslant b-i) \qquad \square$$

Problem 3.17 Consider the random walk in which the steps are independently distributed like a continuous rv X, where X has density $p(x)$ ($-\infty < x < \infty$). Find an integral equation for $F_z(s) = \mathrm{E}_{T|Z_0=z}\, s^T$, where rv T is the number of steps before absorption, if the process starts at z ($-a < z < b$).

Solution. Exactly as in Problem 3.16,

$$F_z(s) = s\left\{ g(z) + \int_{-a}^{b} p(y-z) F_y(s)\, dy \right\} \quad (-a < z < b)$$

where

$$g(z) = \mathrm{pr}(X \leqslant -a-z \quad \text{or} \quad X \geqslant b-z) \qquad \square$$

EXERCISES

1. A particle at each unit time point makes a step to the right with probability p, a step to the left with probability q, or no step at all with probability $r = 1-p-q$. Find the pgf, $G_n(s)$, for the position, Z_n, of the particle after time n if initially it is in position 0. Find the mean and variance of this distribution. Show that

$$G^*(s, t) = \sum_{n=0}^{\infty} G_n(s) t^n = s/\{-ps^2 t + s(1-tr) - tq\}$$

2. Consider a particle which takes an unrestricted random walk as in Problem 3.1. Suppose that the walk has positive drift ($\lambda = q/p < 1$) and that the particle starts in state 0. Use Problem 3.10 to find the distribution of rv W, where $-W$ is the leftmost point the particle reaches.

3. Consider the special case of Problem 3.11 in which $a = 1$ and $p = q = \frac{1}{2}$. Expand $F_{10}(s)$ in powers of s to obtain a formula for $p_k = \mathrm{pr}(T_{10} = k)$. Evaluate p_k for $k = 1, 2, \ldots, 5$. Describe a coin-tossing experiment by which this process can be realised, and carry out 10 realisations.

33

4. A programmed learning text offers three alternative answers to each question. One of the answers is correct and scores two marks. The student selecting this answer can proceed immediately to the next question. Another of the answers carries one mark. The student selecting it can proceed to the next question only after a unit of further reading. The third answer carries no marks, and the student selecting it must undertake two units of further reading before proceeding to the next question. If the student makes a random and independent choice of answer to each question, what is the pgf for the total number of units of further reading he must do before he selects an answer which carries two marks?

5. Solve Problem 3.14 for the general impenetrable barrier having parameter θ.

6. Solve Problem 3.14 for the case in which $p = 1 - \theta$, $q = \theta$ and the impenetrable barrier also has parameter θ.

Chapter 4
Markov Chains

4.1 Definitions A *Markov chain* (abbreviation: MC) is a Markov process $\{Z_n : n \in T\}$ with a discrete time parameter space T, and a finite or countably infinite state space S. We take, without losing generality, both S and T to be subsets of integers. The time-independent *transition probabilities* of a MC are

$$p_{ij}^{(n)} = \text{pr}(Z_{m+n} = j \mid Z_m = i) \quad (i, j \in S)$$

(independent of m). For example, for the unrestricted random walk,

$$p_{ij}^{(1)} = \begin{cases} p & (j = i+1) \\ 1-p & (j = i-1) \\ 0 & (\text{otherwise}) \end{cases}$$

By convention we write p_{ij} for $p_{ij}^{(1)}$. The *one-step transition matrix* (or just *transition matrix*) is the matrix

$$\mathbf{P} = (p_{ij}) \quad (i, j \in S)$$

Now $p_{ij} \geqslant 0$, $\sum_{j \in S} p_{ij} = 1$; the first because the p_{ij} are probabilities, the second because, given $Z_0 = i$, Z_1 must be in some state j of S. For the same reasons the elements of the *n-step transition matrix*

$$\mathbf{P}^{(n)} = (p_{ij}^{(n)}) \quad (i, j \in S)$$

satisfy

$$p_{ij}^{(n)} \geqslant 0, \qquad \sum_{j \in S} p_{ij}^{(n)} = 1$$

We call matrices with these properties—that is, square with nonnegative elements and unit row sums—*stochastic matrices*.

Problem 4.1 What is the transition matrix of the MC $\{Z_n\}$ where each Z_n is independently distributed as rv Z, which has distribution $\text{pr}(Z = k) = p_k$ $(k = 0, 1, 2, \ldots)$?

Solution.

$$p_{ij} = \text{pr}(Z_1 = j \mid Z_0 = i) = \text{pr}(Z_1 = j) \quad (\text{by independence})$$
$$= p_j$$

Therefore

$$
\mathbf{P} = \begin{array}{c} \\ i = 0 \\ i = 1 \\ i = 2 \\ \vdots \end{array}
\begin{array}{ccc}
j = 0 & j = 1 & j = 2 \quad \ldots \\
\left(\begin{array}{ccc}
p_0 & p_1 & p_2 \quad \cdots \\
p_0 & p_1 & p_2 \quad \cdots \\
p_0 & p_1 & p_2 \quad \cdots \\
\vdots & \vdots & \vdots
\end{array}\right)
\end{array}
$$

$\square$

Problem 4.2 What is the transition matrix of the MC $\{Z_n\}$ where $Z_n = Z_{n-1} + X_n$ (see equation 3.2), and the steps X_n are independently distributed as rv X, which has distribution $\mathrm{pr}(X = k) = p_k (k = 0, 1, 2, \ldots)$? What if X has distribution $\mathrm{pr}(X = k) = q_k (k = \ldots, -1, 0, 1, 2, \ldots)$?

Solution.

$$p_{ij} = \mathrm{pr}(Z_1 = j \,|\, Z_0 = i) = \mathrm{pr}(Z_1 - Z_0 = j - i \,|\, Z_0 = i)$$
$$= \mathrm{pr}(X_1 = j - i) \quad \text{(since } Z_0 \text{ and } X_1 \text{ are independent)}$$
$$= \begin{cases} p_{j-i} & (j = i, i+1, i+2, \ldots) \\ 0 & (j = 0, 1, 2, \ldots, i-1) \end{cases}$$

or $\qquad\qquad q_{j-i} \quad (j = \ldots, -1, 0, 1, 2, \ldots)$

so

$$
\begin{array}{c}
\quad\quad j=0 \quad j=1 \quad j=2 \quad j=3 \quad \ldots \\
\mathbf{P} = \begin{array}{r} i=0 \\ i=1 \\ i=2 \\ i=3 \\ \vdots \end{array}
\left(
\begin{array}{ccccc}
p_0 & p_1 & p_2 & p_3 & \cdots \\
0 & p_0 & p_1 & p_2 & \cdots \\
0 & 0 & p_0 & p_1 & \cdots \\
0 & 0 & 0 & p_0 & \cdots \\
\vdots & \vdots & \vdots & \vdots &
\end{array}
\right)
\end{array}
$$

or

$$
\begin{array}{c}
\quad\quad \ldots \quad j=-2 \quad j=-1 \quad j=0 \quad j=1 \quad \ldots \\
\begin{array}{r} i=-1 \\ i=0 \\ i=1 \\ i=2 \\ \vdots \end{array}
\left(
\begin{array}{ccccc}
\cdots & q_{-1} & q_0 & q_1 & q_2 & \cdots \\
\cdots & q_{-2} & q_{-1} & q_0 & q_1 & \cdots \\
\cdots & q_{-3} & q_{-2} & q_{-1} & q_0 & \cdots \\
\cdots & q_{-4} & q_{-3} & q_{-2} & q_{-1} & \cdots \\
& \vdots & \vdots & \vdots & \vdots &
\end{array}
\right)
\end{array}
$$
□

Problem 4.3 A rat is put in the maze illustrated in Figure 4.1. At each time instant it changes room, choosing its exit at random. What is the transition matrix of the MC $\{Z_n\}$, where Z_n is the room the rat is occupying during $(n, n+1)$?

Solution.

$$
\begin{array}{c}
\quad\quad 1 \quad 2 \quad 3 \quad 4 \quad 5 \quad 6 \\
\begin{array}{r} 1 \\ 2 \\ 3 \\ 4 \\ 5 \\ 6 \end{array}
\left(
\begin{array}{cccccc}
0 & \frac{1}{2} & 0 & \frac{1}{2} & 0 & 0 \\
\frac{1}{3} & 0 & \frac{1}{3} & 0 & \frac{1}{3} & 0 \\
0 & 1 & 0 & 0 & 0 & 0 \\
1 & 0 & 0 & 0 & 0 & 0 \\
0 & \frac{1}{2} & 0 & 0 & 0 & \frac{1}{2} \\
0 & 0 & 0 & 0 & 1 & 0
\end{array}
\right)
\end{array}
$$
□

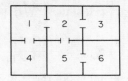

Figure 4.1

Problem 4.4 Show that the factory described in Problem 1.7 can be analysed as an MC.

Solution. Exercise 1 of Chapter 1 asked for a list of the possible transitions between the states of the factory. We list the transitions here, with their corresponding probabilities. They were found by considering the event at the factory which caused its state to change. Let $q = 1 - p$.

Transition from state	i:	0	0	1	1	2	2	3	otherwise
to state	j:	0	2	0	2	1	3	2	
with probability	p_{ij}:	q	p	q	p	q	p	1	0

i.e. transition matrix

$$\mathbf{P} = (p_{ij}) = \begin{matrix} & \begin{matrix} 0 & 1 & 2 & 3 \end{matrix} \\ \begin{matrix} 0 \\ 1 \\ 2 \\ 3 \end{matrix} & \begin{pmatrix} q & 0 & p & 0 \\ q & 0 & p & 0 \\ 0 & q & 0 & p \\ 0 & 0 & 1 & 0 \end{pmatrix} \end{matrix}$$

□

Problem 4.5 Consider the library book loan process described in Problem 1.5. Suppose that the times in weeks it takes the reader to read library books are independent rvs having distribution function $F(t)$. If $\{F(j) : j = 0, 1, 2, \ldots\}$ is a sequence with $F(j) < F(j+1)$ show that the process is an MC, and find its transition matrix.

Solution. Let the time to read a book be an rv T. A book is exchanged if and only if the reader finished it during the previous week. This has the Markov property, and so the process is an MC. The only possible transitions are i to 0 or to $i+1$ ($i = 0, 1, 2, \ldots$), so $p_{ij} = 0$ ($j \neq 0, i+1$), and $p_{i0} + p_{i,i+1} = 1$. Now $\mathrm{pr}(Z_n = i) = \mathrm{pr}(T > i) = 1 - F(i)$, and

$$p_{i,i+1} = \mathrm{pr}(Z_{n+1} = i+1 \mid Z_n = i) = \mathrm{pr}(T > i+1 \mid T > i)$$

$$= \frac{\mathrm{pr}(T > i+1, T > i)}{\mathrm{pr}(T > i)} = \frac{\mathrm{pr}(T > i+1)}{\mathrm{pr}(T > i)} = \frac{1 - F(i+1)}{1 - F(i)}$$

$$(i = 0, 1, 2, \ldots)$$

where $F(0) = 0$; and $p_{i,i+1} < 1$ since $\{F(j)\}$ is a monotone increasing sequence. Therefore

$$p_{io} = 1 - p_{i,i+1} = \frac{F(i+1) - F(i)}{1 - F(i)}$$

These probabilities are the elements of the transition matrix. □

Problem 4.6 Consider a time-dependent MC $\{X_n : n = 0, 1, 2, \ldots\}$ defined on the state space $\{0, 1\}$. If $\mathrm{pr}(X_0 = 1) = \theta_0$ and $\mathrm{pr}(X_m = 1 \mid X_{m-1} = 1) = \theta_m (m = 1, 2, \ldots)$, show that $\{Z_n : n = 0, 1, 2, \ldots\}$, where $Z_n = X_0 X_1 \ldots X_n$, is also a time-dependent MC, and determine the marginal distribution of Z_n.

Solution.

$$Z_n = Z_{n-1} X_n, \qquad Z_0 = X_0$$

If $Z_{n-1} = 0$, then $Z_n = 0$ (so state 0 is an absorbing barrier of the time-dependent random walk $\{Z_n\}$ on $\{0, 1\}$). If $Z_{n-1} = 1$, then $X_m = 1$ $(m = 0, 1, \ldots, n-1)$, and by the Markov property of $\{X_n\}$

$$\mathrm{pr}(Z_n = 1 \mid Z_{n-1} = 1) = \mathrm{pr}(X_n = 1 \mid X_{n-1} = 1) = \theta_n$$

and

$$\mathrm{pr}(Z_n = 0 \mid Z_{n-1} = 1) = 1 - \theta_n$$

Therefore, given Z_{n-1}, we need no further information in predicting Z_n, so $\{Z_n\}$ is an MC.

Z_n is a Bernoulli rv (Exercise 3 of Chapter 2). Also

$$\mathrm{E}_{Z_n \mid Z_{n-1} = z_{n-1}} Z_n = \begin{cases} 0 & (Z_{n-1} = 0) \\ \mathrm{E}_{Z_n \mid Z_{n-1} = 1} Z_n = \theta_n & (Z_{n-1} = 1) \end{cases}$$
$$= \theta_n Z_{n-1}$$

Therefore, the probability of success,

$$\begin{aligned}
\mathrm{pr}(Z_n = 1) &= \mathrm{E}_{Z_n} Z_n = \mathrm{E}_{Z_{n-1}} \mathrm{E}_{Z_n \mid Z_{n-1} = z_{n-1}} Z_n \\
&= \mathrm{E}_{Z_{n-1}} \theta_n Z_{n-1} = \theta_n \mathrm{pr}(Z_{n-1} = 1) = \theta_n \{\theta_{n-1} \mathrm{pr}(Z_{n-2} = 1)\} \\
&= \ldots = \theta_n \theta_{n-1} \ldots \theta_1 \mathrm{pr}(Z_0 = 1) = \theta_n \ldots \theta_1 \mathrm{pr}(X_0 = 1) \\
&= \theta_0 \theta_1 \ldots \theta_n
\end{aligned}$$
□

Consider an MC $\{Z_n : n = 0, 1, 2, \ldots\}$ having time-independent transition matrix $\mathbf{P}$. If the distribution of the initial state is $\mathrm{pr}(Z_0 = i) = p_i$ $(i = 0, 1, 2, \ldots)$, then by applying the Markov property to equation 2.23 we obtain the joint distribution of $Z_0, Z_1, \ldots, Z_n$:

$$\mathrm{pr}(Z_0 = i_0, \quad Z_1 = i_1, \quad \ldots, \quad Z_n = i_n) = p_{i_0} p_{i_0 i_1} p_{i_1 i_2} \ldots p_{i_{n-1} i_n} \quad (4.1)$$

Let us denote $\mathrm{pr}(\cdot \mid Z_0 = i)$ by $\mathrm{pr}_i(\cdot)$, then $\mathrm{pr}_i(Z_1 = k) = p_{ik}$, and by the Markov property and time independence

$$\text{pr}_i(Z_2 = j \mid Z_1 = k) = \text{pr}(Z_2 = j \mid Z_1 = k) = p_{kj}$$

After its first step the particle must be in one of the states of S. Therefore, by equation 2.12,

$$p_{ij}^{(2)} = \text{pr}_i(Z_2 = j) = \sum_{k \in S} \text{pr}_i(Z_2 = j \mid Z_1 = k)\text{pr}_i(Z_1 = k) = \sum_{k \in S} p_{ik}p_{kj}$$

In matrix notation the right side is the (i,j) element of $\mathbf{PP} = \mathbf{P}^2$, where $\mathbf{P}$ is the one-step transition matrix. The two-step transition matrix $(p_{ij}^{(2)})$ is thus $\mathbf{P}^2$. Similarly $(p_{ij}^{(3)}) = \mathbf{P}^3$, and so on. In general

$$p_{ij}^{(m+n)} = \sum_{k \in S} p_{ik}^{(m)} p_{kj}^{(n)}$$

This is called the *Chapman–Kolmogorov equation*. In matrix notation

$$\mathbf{P}^{m+n} = \mathbf{P}^m \mathbf{P}^n$$

We can define $\mathbf{P}^0$ in a natural way to be $\mathbf{I} = (\delta_{ij})$, the identity matrix, where δ_{ij} is the Kronecker delta $(= 1 \text{ if } i = j, = 0 \text{ if } i \neq j)$.

Problem 4.7 Consider an MC $\{X_n : n = 0, 1, 2, \ldots\}$ with finite state space $S = \{0, 1, \ldots, s\}$ and transition matrix $\mathbf{P} = (p_{ij})$. Suppose that the MC has been *thinned* according to the matrix $\mathbf{\Gamma} = (\gamma_{ij})$. That is, given $X_n = i$ and $X_{n+1} = j$, we delete X_{n+1} from the realisation with probability γ_{ij} and retain it with probability $1 - \gamma_{ij}$. This thinning has the Markov property. Show that the *thinned process* $\{Z_n : n = 0, 1, 2, \ldots\}$, where $Z_0 = X_0$ is an MC, and find its transition matrix $\mathbf{P}^* = (p_{ij}^*)$.

Solution. Each Z_k of the thinned process is an X_j of the MC. Therefore

$$\text{pr}(Z_{k+1} = j \mid Z_0 = i_0, \quad Z_1 = i_1, \quad \ldots, \quad Z_k = i_k)$$
$$= \text{pr}(X_{n_{k+1}} = j \mid X_0 = i_0, \quad X_{n_1} = i_1, \quad \ldots, \quad X_{n_k} = i_k) \quad \text{for some}$$
$$\text{sequence } n_1, n_2, \ldots, n_{k+1}$$
$$= \text{pr}(X_{n_{k+1}} = j \mid X_{n_k} = i_k) \quad \text{by the Markov property of } \{X_n\}$$
$$= \text{pr}(Z_{k+1} = j \mid Z_k = i_k)$$

so $\{Z_k\}$ is an MC.

We consider a decomposition based on the first step, whether or not it is deleted. Let

$$Y = \begin{cases} 1 & \text{if the first step is deleted} \\ 0 & \text{otherwise} \end{cases}$$

Then

$$\mathbb{E}_{Z_1 \mid Z_0 = i} s^{Z_1} = \mathbb{E}_{X_1, Y, Z_1 \mid Z_0 = i} s^{Z_1}$$
$$= \mathbb{E}_{X_1 \mid Z_0 = i} \, \mathbb{E}_{Y \mid X_1 = X_1, Z_0 = i} \, \mathbb{E}_{Z_1 \mid X_1 = X_1, Y = Y, Z_0 = i} s^{Z_1}$$

We pick out the coefficient of s^j, i.e.

$$p_{ij}^* = \text{pr}(Z_1 = j \mid Z_0 = i)$$
$$= \text{E}_{X_1 \mid Z_0 = i} \text{E}_{Y \mid X_1 = X_1, Z_0 = i} \text{pr}(Z_1 = j \mid X_1 = X_1, \ Y = Y, \ Z_0 = i) \quad (4.2)$$
Now
$$\text{pr}(X_1 = k \mid Z_0 = i) = p_{ik}$$
and
$$\text{E}_{Y \mid X_1 = k, Z_0 = i} Y = \text{pr}(Y = 1 \mid X_1 = k, \ Z_0 = i) = \gamma_{ik} \quad (4.3)$$
Also, by the Markov property, if $X_1 = k$, then it is as though the thinned process starts again from k. Therefore
$$\text{pr}(Z_1 = j \mid X_1 = k, \quad Y = 0, \quad Z_0 = i) = \delta_{kj} \quad \text{(the Kronecker delta)}$$
and
$$\text{pr}(Z_1 = j \mid X_1 = k, \quad Y = 1, \quad Z_0 = i) = \text{pr}(Z_1 = j \mid Z_0 = k) = p_{kj}^*$$
so
$$\text{pr}(Z_1 = j \mid X_1 = k, \quad Y = y, \quad Z_0 = i) = (1-y)\delta_{kj} + y p_{kj}^* \quad (y = 0, 1)$$
By equation 4.2
$$p_{ij}^* = \text{E}_{X_1 \mid Z_0 = i} \text{E}_{Y \mid X_1 = X_1, Z_0 = i}\{(1-Y)\delta_{X_1 j} + Y p_{X_1 j}^*\}$$
$$= \text{E}_{X_1 \mid Z_0 = i}\{(1-\gamma_{iX_1})\delta_{X_1 j} + \gamma_{iX_1} p_{X_1 j}^*\} \quad \text{(by 4.3)}$$
$$= \sum_{k \in S} p_{ik}\{(1-\gamma_{ik})\delta_{kj} + \gamma_{ik} p_{kj}^*\} = p_{ij}(1-\gamma_{ij}) + \sum_{k \in S} p_{ik}\gamma_{ik} p_{kj}^*$$
$$= p_{ij} - q_{ij} + \sum_{k \in S} q_{ik} p_{kj}^*, \quad \text{where } \mathbf{Q} = (q_{ij}) = (p_{ij}\gamma_{ij})$$
i.e.
$$\mathbf{P}^* = \mathbf{P} - \mathbf{Q} + \mathbf{Q}\mathbf{P}^*$$
i.e.
$$(\mathbf{I} - \mathbf{Q})\mathbf{P}^* = \mathbf{P} - \mathbf{Q}$$
Therefore
$$\mathbf{P}^* = (\mathbf{I} - \mathbf{Q})^{-1}(\mathbf{P} - \mathbf{Q}) \qquad \square$$

4.2 Equilibrium distributions We seek the limiting form of $\mathbf{P}^n$ as $n \to \infty$, if the limit exists.

Problem 4.8 Find $\Pi = \lim_{n \to \infty} \mathbf{P}^n$ for a time-independent MC having state space $S = \{0, 1\}$.

Solution. A realisation of this process will be a sequence of 0s and 1s. The transition matrix $\mathbf{P}$ must be of the form
$$\mathbf{P} = \begin{pmatrix} 1-\alpha & \alpha \\ \beta & 1-\beta \end{pmatrix} \quad (0 \leqslant \alpha, \beta \leqslant 1)$$

We first consider the special cases in which α or β are 0 or 1. If $\alpha = \beta = 0$ the particle stays in its initial state so

40

$$\Pi = \begin{pmatrix} 1 & 0 \\ 0 & 1 \end{pmatrix} = I$$

i.e. both states are absorbing. If $\alpha = 1$ and $\beta = 1$, the particle on alternate steps goes from state 0 to state 1 and back again, so the MC $\{Z_n\}$ is such that $Z_{2n} = Z_0$ and $Z_{2n+1} = 1 - Z_0$, so there is no limiting distribution. If $0 < \alpha \leq 1$ and $\beta = 0$, state 1 is absorbing, i.e. when the particle reaches state 1 it stays there, so

$$\Pi = \begin{pmatrix} 0 & 1 \\ 0 & 1 \end{pmatrix}$$

Similarly if $\alpha = 0$ and $0 < \beta \leq 1$, $\Pi = \begin{pmatrix} 1 & 0 \\ 1 & 0 \end{pmatrix}$. For the case $0 < \alpha, \beta < 1$, consider matrix

$$\Lambda = \begin{pmatrix} 1 & 0 \\ 0 & \lambda \end{pmatrix}$$

where $\lambda = 1 - \alpha - \beta$. (1 and λ are the eigenvalues of $\mathbf{P}$.) Then

$$\Lambda^n = \begin{pmatrix} 1 & 0 \\ 0 & \lambda^n \end{pmatrix} \rightarrow \begin{pmatrix} 1 & 0 \\ 0 & 0 \end{pmatrix}$$

as $n \rightarrow \infty$, since $|\lambda| < 1$. Now consider matrix

$$\mathbf{R} = \begin{pmatrix} 1 & -\alpha \\ 1 & \beta \end{pmatrix} \quad \left(\mathbf{R}^{-1} = \frac{1}{\alpha + \beta} \begin{pmatrix} \beta & \alpha \\ -1 & 1 \end{pmatrix} \right)$$

Then

$$\mathbf{P} = \begin{pmatrix} 1-\alpha & \alpha \\ \beta & 1-\beta \end{pmatrix} = \mathbf{R}\Lambda\mathbf{R}^{-1}$$

Therefore

$$\mathbf{P}^2 = \mathbf{R}\Lambda\mathbf{R}^{-1}\mathbf{R}\Lambda\mathbf{R}^{-1} = \mathbf{R}\Lambda(\mathbf{R}^{-1}\mathbf{R})\Lambda\mathbf{R}^{-1} = \mathbf{R}(\Lambda I\Lambda)\mathbf{R}^{-1} = \mathbf{R}\Lambda^2\mathbf{R}^{-1},$$

and

$$\mathbf{P}^3 = \mathbf{R}\Lambda^2\mathbf{R}^{-1}\mathbf{R}\Lambda\mathbf{R}^{-1} = \mathbf{R}\Lambda^3\mathbf{R}^{-1}$$

and in general

$$\mathbf{P}^n = \mathbf{R}\Lambda^n\mathbf{R}^{-1} \rightarrow \mathbf{R}\begin{pmatrix} 1 & 0 \\ 0 & 0 \end{pmatrix}\mathbf{R}^{-1} = \frac{1}{\alpha+\beta}\begin{pmatrix} 1 & -\alpha \\ 1 & \beta \end{pmatrix}\begin{pmatrix} 1 & 0 \\ 0 & 0 \end{pmatrix}\begin{pmatrix} \beta & \alpha \\ -1 & 1 \end{pmatrix}$$

$$= \frac{1}{\alpha+\beta}\begin{pmatrix} \beta & \alpha \\ \beta & \alpha \end{pmatrix} = \begin{pmatrix} 1 \\ 1 \end{pmatrix}\left(\frac{\beta}{\alpha+\beta} \quad \frac{\alpha}{\alpha+\beta}\right) = \mathbf{1}\boldsymbol{\pi}' \text{ as } n \rightarrow \infty$$

where $\pi_0 = \beta/(\alpha+\beta)$, $\pi_1 = \alpha/(\alpha+\beta)$ forms a probability distribution. That is, $p_{ij}^{(n)} \rightarrow \pi_j$ independent of the initial state i, so π_j is the equilibrium probability of the particle being in state j. $\quad\square$

In general, if a limiting matrix Π exists, then $\Pi = \mathbf{1}\boldsymbol{\pi}'$ where $\mathbf{1}$ is a column vector of 1s and π is the equilibrium distribution of the MC. To find π' we do not need to construct a matrix $\mathbf{R}$ as above. Since

$$\mathbf{P}^{n+1} = \mathbf{P}^n\mathbf{P}$$

by letting $n \to \infty$ we obtain

$$\mathbf{1}\pi' = \mathbf{1}\pi'\mathbf{P}$$

so

$$\pi' = \pi'\mathbf{P} \tag{4.4}$$

This is a set of simultaneous equations for π_j (i.e. π' is the left eigenvector of $\mathbf{P}$ corresponding to the eigenvalue 1).

Problem 4.9 Find the equilibrium distribution of the two-state MC having transition matrix $\begin{pmatrix} 1-\alpha & \alpha \\ \beta & 1-\beta \end{pmatrix}$ $(0 < \alpha, \beta < 1)$.

Solution. This is, of course, Problem 4.8. We solve $\pi' = \pi'\mathbf{P}$ for π'. Here

$$(\pi_0 \; \pi_1) = (\pi_0 \; \pi_1)\begin{pmatrix} 1-\alpha & \alpha \\ \beta & 1-\beta \end{pmatrix} = (\pi_0(1-\alpha)+\pi_1\beta, \; \pi_0\alpha+\pi_1(1-\beta))$$

Therefore

$$\pi_0\alpha = \pi_1\beta$$

Since $\pi_0 + \pi_1 = 1$, we must have $\pi_0 = \beta/(\alpha+\beta), \pi_1 = \alpha/(\alpha+\beta)$ ☐

Problem 4.10 In a random walk on states $\{-2, -1, 0, 1, 2\}$, if at time n the particle is in state i $(i = -1, 0, 1)$, then at time $n+1$ it is equally likely to be in $i-1$ or $i+1$; and if it is at time n in state -2 or 2, then at time $n+1$ it is equally likely to be in -1, 0 or 1. Write down the transition matrix of this MC, and find its equilibrium distribution.

Solution.

$$\mathbf{P} = \begin{array}{c} \\ -2 \\ -1 \\ 0 \\ 1 \\ 2 \end{array}\begin{pmatrix} 0 & \frac{1}{3} & \frac{1}{3} & \frac{1}{3} & 0 \\ \frac{1}{2} & 0 & \frac{1}{2} & 0 & 0 \\ 0 & \frac{1}{2} & 0 & \frac{1}{2} & 0 \\ 0 & 0 & \frac{1}{2} & 0 & \frac{1}{2} \\ 0 & \frac{1}{3} & \frac{1}{3} & \frac{1}{3} & 0 \end{pmatrix}$$

$$\begin{array}{ccccc} -2 & -1 & 0 & 1 & 2 \end{array}$$

We wish to solve $\pi' = \pi'\mathbf{P}$ for $\pi' = (\pi_{-2} \; \pi_{-1} \; \pi_0 \; \pi_1 \; \pi_2)$. Clearly by symmetry $\pi_{-2} = \pi_2, \pi_{-1} = \pi_1$. Then

$$\pi_0 = \tfrac{1}{3}\pi_2 + \tfrac{1}{2}\pi_1 + \tfrac{1}{2}\pi_1 + \tfrac{1}{3}\pi_2 \tag{4.5}$$

$$\pi_1 = \tfrac{1}{3}\pi_2 + \tfrac{1}{2}\pi_0 + \tfrac{1}{3}\pi_2 \tag{4.6}$$

$$\pi_2 = \tfrac{1}{2}\pi_1 \tag{4.7}$$

We have further that

$$1 = \pi_{-2} + \pi_{-1} + \pi_0 + \pi_1 + \pi_2 = \pi_0 + 2\pi_1 + 2\pi_2 \qquad (4.8)$$

Substituting (4.7) into (4.5) or (4.6) gives

$$\pi_0 = \tfrac{4}{3}\pi_1$$

and substituting this and (4.7) into (4.8) gives $\pi_1 = 3/13$, then

$$\pi' = (\tfrac{3}{26}\ \tfrac{3}{13}\ \tfrac{4}{13}\ \tfrac{3}{13}\ \tfrac{3}{26}) \qquad \square$$

4.3 Applications

Problem 4.11 *The Ehrenfest model of gas diffusion through a porous membrane.* Two cells, A and B, contain together $2a$ molecules of gas. At each time instant a molecule is chosen at random from the $2a$, and if the chosen molecule is from cell A it is put into cell B, and if it is from cell B it is put into cell A. Find the transition matrix for the MC $\{X_n : n = 0, 1, 2, \ldots\}$, where rv X_n is the number of molecules in cell A at time instant n. Determine a differential-difference equation for

$$F_n(s) = E_{X_n | X_0 = i} s^{X_n}$$

for a fixed i. Find the equilibrium distribution of the MC. Determine $M_n = E_{X_n | X_0 = i} X_n.$

TABLE 4.1

$X_n \to X_{n+1}$		Probability	Comment
k	$k+1$	$(2a - k)/2a$	This is the probability of selecting a molecule from B ($k = 1, 2, \ldots, 2a - 1$)
k	$k-1$	$k/2a$	This is the probability of selecting a molecule from A
0	1	1	State 0 is a reflecting barrier
$2a$	$2a - 1$	1	State $2a$ is a reflecting barrier

Solution. From Table 4.1 of possible transitions, we find that

$$p_{ij} = \text{pr}(X_{n+1} = j \mid X_n = i)$$

$$= \begin{cases} (2a-i)/(2a) & (j = i+1; \quad i = 0, 1, \ldots, 2a-1) \\ i/(2a) & (j = i-1; \quad i = 1, 2, \ldots, 2a) \\ 0 & (\text{otherwise}). \end{cases}$$

We shall write α for $2a$. By a decomposition based on the last step

$$F_{n+1}(s) = \mathrm{E}_{X_{n+1}\mid X_0 = i} s^{X_{n+1}} = \mathrm{E}_{X_n\mid X_0 = i} \mathrm{E}_{X_{n+1}\mid X_n = X_n, X_0 = i} s^{X_{n+1}}$$

$$= \mathrm{E}_{X_n\mid X_0 = i} \mathrm{E}_{X_{n+1}\mid X_n = X_n} s^{X_{n+1}}$$

by the Markov property. Now

$$\mathrm{E}_{X_{n+1}\mid X_n = k} s^{X_{n+1}} = \begin{cases} s^{k-1}\left(\dfrac{k}{\alpha}\right) + s^{k+1}\left(\dfrac{\alpha-k}{\alpha}\right) & (k = 1, 2, \ldots, \alpha-1) \\ s & (k = 0) \\ s^{\alpha-1} & (k = \alpha) \end{cases}$$

$$= \frac{1}{\alpha}(1 - s^2)ks^{k-1} + s^{k+1} \quad (k = 0, 1, \ldots, \alpha)$$

Therefore

$$\alpha F_{n+1}(s) = (1 - s^2)\mathrm{E}_{X_n\mid X_0 = i} X_n s^{X_n - 1} + \alpha s \mathrm{E}_{X_n\mid X_0 = i} s^{X_n}$$

$$= (1 - s^2)\frac{d}{ds} F_n(s) + \alpha s\, F_n(s) \tag{4.9}$$

Let $F_n(s) \to F(s)$ as $n \to \infty$; then

$$\alpha F = (1 - s^2)F' + \alpha s F,$$

i.e.

$$\gamma F = (1 + s)\frac{dF}{ds}.$$

Therefore

$$F(s) = \{c(1+s)\}^\alpha, \quad \text{where } c \text{ is a constant.}$$

But $F(1) = \mathrm{E}1 = 1 = (2c)^\alpha$

Therefore

$$c = \tfrac{1}{2}$$

Therefore

$$F(s) = \sum_{k=0}^{\alpha} p_{ik}^{(\infty)} s^k = \frac{1}{2^\alpha}(1 + s)^\alpha = \frac{1}{2^\alpha} \sum_{k=0}^{\alpha} \binom{\alpha}{k} s^\alpha$$

Therefore

$$p_{ik}^{(\infty)} = \binom{\alpha}{k}\frac{1}{2^\alpha} = \binom{2a}{k}\frac{1}{2^{2a}} \quad (k = 0, 1, \ldots, 2a)$$

i.e. the equilibrium distribution of $\{X_n\}$ is $\text{Bin}(2a, \tfrac{1}{2})$.

44

If we set $s = 1$ in equation 4.9 and put $M_n = F'_n(1)$ we obtain the identity $\alpha = \alpha$. However, if we differentiate equation 4.9 we obtain

$$\alpha F'_{n+1}(s) = (1-s^2)F''_n(s) + (\alpha-2)s\,F'_n(s) + \alpha F_n(s)$$

Now, if we set $s = 1$ and $\alpha = 2a$, we obtain
$$2aM_{n+1} = (2a-2)M_n + 2a$$

i.e.
$$M_{n+1} - a = \left(1 - \frac{1}{a}\right)(M_n - a)$$

Therefore
$$M_n - a = \left(1 - \frac{1}{a}\right)(M_{n-1} - a) = \left(1 - \frac{1}{a}\right)^2 (M_{n-2} - a) = \left(1 - \frac{1}{a}\right)^n (M_0 - a)$$

i.e.
$$M_n = a + \left(1 - \frac{1}{a}\right)^n (i - a). \qquad \square$$

Problem 4.12 *A simple queue model.* A single server at time instants $1, 2, \ldots$ serves a customer, if any are waiting. Suppose that in time interval $(n, n+1)$ X_n customers arrive, where $\{X_n\}$ is a sequence of independent rvs, each distributed as rv X, where $\mathrm{pr}(X = k) = p_k$ $(k = 0, 1, 2, \ldots)$. If rv Z_n is the number of customers present (including the one being served) at time instant n, show that $\{Z_n : n = 0, 1, 2, \ldots\}$ is an MC. Find its transition matrix and equilibrium distribution.

Solution. We prove that $\{Z_n\}$ is an MC by showing that Z_{n+1} depends only on Z_n and X_n and on no earlier information. The number of customers present at time $n+1$ is the number present at time n, less the one served at time n, plus the number of new arrivals in $(n, n+1)$, i.e.

$$Z_{n+1} = \begin{cases} Z_n - 1 + X_n & (Z_n = 1, 2, \ldots) \\ X_n & (Z_n = 0) \end{cases}$$
$$= Z_n - \Delta_n + X_n \tag{4.10}$$

where
$$\Delta_n = \begin{cases} 1 & (Z_n = 1, 2, \ldots) \\ 0 & (Z_n = 0) \end{cases}$$

Therefore
$$p_{0j} = \mathrm{pr}(Z_{n+1} = j \mid Z_n = 0) = \mathrm{pr}(X_n = j) = p_j \quad (j = 0, 1, 2, \ldots)$$
and for $i \neq 0$
$$p_{ij} = \mathrm{pr}(Z_{n+1} = j \mid Z_n = i) = \mathrm{pr}(Z_n - 1 + X_n = j \mid Z_n = i)$$
$$= \mathrm{pr}(X_n = j - i + 1) = \begin{cases} p_{j-i+1} & (j = i-1, i, i+1, \ldots) \\ 0 & (j = 0, 1, \ldots, i-2) \end{cases}$$

i.e.

$$\mathbf{P} = \begin{array}{c} \\ 0 \\ 1 \\ 2 \\ 3 \\ \vdots \end{array} \begin{array}{cccccc} 0 & 1 & 2 & 3 & \cdots \\ \left(\begin{array}{ccccc} p_0 & p_1 & p_2 & p_3 & \cdots \\ p_0 & p_1 & p_2 & p_3 & \cdots \\ 0 & p_0 & p_1 & p_2 & \cdots \\ 0 & 0 & p_0 & p_1 & \cdots \\ \vdots & \vdots & \vdots & \vdots & \end{array} \right) \end{array}$$

We solve $\pi' = \pi'\mathbf{P}$ for $\pi' = (\pi_0 \ \pi_1 \ \pi_2 \ \ldots)$ and find

$$\pi_k = \pi_0 p_k + \sum_{j=1}^{k+1} \pi_j \, p_{k+1-j} \quad (k = 0, 1, 2, \ldots) \tag{4.11}$$

These may be solved successively to find π_k in terms of π_0. Then $\Sigma \, \pi_k = 1$ will give the value of π_0. Alternatively, let us define pgfs

$$\Pi(s) = \sum_{k=0}^{\infty} \pi_k s^k, \qquad P(s) = \sum_{k=0}^{\infty} p_k s^k;$$

then $P(s) = Es^x$ is known. We call $EX = \rho$ the *traffic intensity* (= ratio of expected number of arrivals to expected number of departures). We multiply equation 4.11 by s^k and sum for $k = 0$ to ∞:

$$\Pi(s) = \pi_0 P(s) + \frac{1}{s} \sum_{k=0}^{\infty} \sum_{j=1}^{k+1} \pi_j s^j p_{k+1-j} s^{k+1-j}$$

$$= \pi_0 P(s) + \frac{1}{s} \sum_{j=1}^{\infty} \pi_j s^j \sum_{r=k+1-j=0}^{\infty} p_r s^r \quad \text{(by changing the order of summation)}$$

$$= \pi_0 P(s) + \frac{1}{s} \{\Pi(s) - \pi_0\} P(s)$$

Therefore

$$\Pi(s) = \frac{\pi_0(1-s)P(s)}{P(s) - s}$$

Now

$$1 = \Pi(1) = \pi_0 \lim_{s \uparrow 1} \frac{(1-s)P(s)}{P(s) - s} = \pi_0 \lim_{s \uparrow 1} \frac{\dfrac{d}{ds}\{(1-s)P(s)\}}{\dfrac{d}{ds}\{P(s) - s\}} \quad \text{(l'Hôpital's rule)}$$

$$= \pi_0 \lim_{s \uparrow 1} \frac{(1-s)P'(s) - P(s)}{P'(s) - 1} = \pi_0 \frac{-1}{\rho - 1}$$

Therefore

$$\pi_0 = 1 - \rho$$

Therefore

$$\Pi(s) = \frac{(1-\rho)(1-s)P(s)}{P(s)-s}$$

The condition for stability (i.e. an equilibrium solution) is $\rho < 1$, because if $\rho = 1$, then $\pi_0 = 0$ so $\Pi(s) = 0$, and if $\rho > 1$, $\pi_0 < 0$, and is not a probability. If $\rho > 1$ the queue size will tend to grow without limit. □

Problem 4.13 Suppose that in the simple queue model there is waiting room for only m customers including the one being served. Customers who arrive to find the waiting room full leave without being served and do not return. What is the transition matrix? Show how to find the equilibrium distribution.

Solution. $Z_{n+1} = \min(Z_n - \Delta_n + X_n, m)$

$$= \begin{cases} Z_n - 1 + X_n & (Z_n = 1, 2, \ldots, m; \quad X_n = 0, 1, \ldots, m+1-Z_n) \\ X_n & (Z_n = 0; \quad X_n = 0, 1, \ldots, m-1) \\ m & \text{(otherwise)} \end{cases}$$

Therefore

$p_{0j} = \mathrm{pr}(Z_{n+1} = j \mid Z_n = 0)$

$$= \begin{cases} \mathrm{pr}(X_n = j) = p_j & (j = 0, 1, \ldots, m-1) \\ \mathrm{pr}(X_n \geqslant m) = p_m + p_{m+1} + \ldots = P_m, & \text{say} \quad (j = m) \\ 0 & \text{(otherwise)} \end{cases}$$

and, for $i = 1, 2, \ldots, m$,

$p_{ij} = \mathrm{pr}(Z_{n+1} = j \mid Z_n = i)$

$$= \begin{cases} \mathrm{pr}(X_n = j+1-i) = p_{j-i+1} & (j = i-1, i, \ldots, m-1) \\ \mathrm{pr}(X_n \geqslant m+1-i) = P_{m+1-i} & (j = m) \\ 0 & \text{(otherwise)} \end{cases}$$

i.e.

$$\mathbf{P}^* = \begin{array}{c} \\ 0 \\ 1 \\ 2 \\ \vdots \\ m \end{array} \begin{array}{cccccc} 0 & 1 & 2 & \ldots & m-1 & m \\ \left(\begin{array}{cccccc} p_0 & p_1 & p_2 & \ldots & p_{m-1} & P_m \\ p_0 & p_1 & p_2 & \ldots & p_{m-1} & P_m \\ 0 & p_0 & p_1 & \ldots & p_{m-2} & P_{m-1} \\ \vdots & \vdots & \vdots & & \vdots & \vdots \\ 0 & 0 & 0 & \ldots & p_0 & P_1 \end{array} \right) \end{array}$$

In solving $\boldsymbol{\pi}^{*\prime} = \boldsymbol{\pi}^{*\prime}\mathbf{P}^*$, the first m equations are the same as in (4.11). Therefore $\pi_j^* = c\pi_j$ $(j = 0, 1, \ldots, m-1)$, where c is a constant. This is because each π_j^* $(j = 0, 1, \ldots, m-1)$ is the same function of π_0^* as π_j is of π_0. The last equation is

$$\pi_m^* = \pi_0^* P_m + \sum_{j=1}^{m} \pi_j^* P_{m+1-j} = \pi_0^* P_m + \sum_{j=1}^{m-1} \pi_j^* P_{m+1-j} + \pi_m^* P_1$$

where $P_m = p_m + p_{m+1} + \dots$. This reduces, where γ_m is known by Problem 4.12, to

$$p_0 \pi_m^* = (1 - P_1)\pi_m^* = c\left(\pi_0 P_m + \sum_{j=1}^{m-1} \pi_j P_{m+1-j}\right) = c\gamma_m \quad \text{say}$$

Now

$$p_0 = p_0 \sum_{j=0}^{m} \pi_j^* = p_0 c \sum_{j=0}^{m-1} \pi_j + c\gamma_m$$

Therefore

$$c = p_0 \bigg/ \left\{ p_0 \sum_{j=1}^{m-1} \pi_j + \gamma_m \right\} \qquad \square$$

Problem 4.14 *The discrete branching process.* Each individual in a population gives rise to X new individuals for the next generation, where rv X has pgf $G(s)$. Individuals reproduce independently of one another and then die. This occurs at the same instant for each individual after a fixed constant lifetime. If the process starts with a single individual, show that $\Pi_n(s)$, the pgf for Z_n, the population size in the nth generation, satisfies recurrence relations

$$\Pi_{n+1}(s) = \Pi_n\{G(s)\}, \qquad \Pi_{n+1}(s) = G\{\Pi_n(s)\} \qquad (4.12)$$

where clearly $\Pi_0(s) = s$ and $\Pi_1(s) = G(s)$.

Solution. We consider decompositions based on the last and the first generations respectively. We can write

$$Z_{n+1} = X_1 + \dots + X_{Z_n} \qquad (4.13)$$

since each of the Z_n individuals in the nth generation has his own family. The family sizes $\{X_i : i = 1, 2, \dots, Z_n\}$ are independently distributed, each with pgf $G(s)$. Then, by Problem 2.14, Z_{n+1} has pgf $\Pi_n\{G(s)\}$.

Alternatively we can consider the populations which grow in the remaining n generations from the $Z_1 = X$ born in the first generation. Then

$$Z_{n+1} = Z_n^{(1)} + \dots + Z_n^{(X)} \qquad (4.14)$$

where the $Z_n^{(i)}$ are independently each distributed like Z_n. Then, again by Problem 2.14, Z_{n+1} has pgf $G\{\Pi_n(s)\}$. $\qquad \square$

Making parents die when they give birth is no restriction since we could have a parent survive as one of its offspring if $G(0) = \mathrm{pr}(X = 0) = 0$. This is because individuals behave independently and alike, so parents and offspring will be indistinguishable. On the other hand, if we have $G(0) > 0$, the number of children is not restricted to one or more, so it will be possible for the population to die out. We then have the problem of determining the chance of extinction.

Problem 4.15 Determine $M_n = EZ_n$ and $V_n = VZ_n$ for the population size in the nth generation.

Solution. $Z_0 = 1$ so $M_0 = 1$ and $V_0 = 0$. From equation 4.13,

$$E_{Z_{n+1}|Z_n=k}Z_{n+1} = E(X_1 + \ldots + X_k) = k\,EX = k\alpha$$

where $\alpha = EX = G'(1)$ is the mean family size. Therefore

$$M_{n+1} = EZ_{n+1} = E_{Z_n}E_{Z_{n+1}|Z_n=Z_n}Z_{n+1} = E_{Z_n}(Z_n\alpha) = \alpha M_n$$

This is a recurrence relation, and obviously

$$M_n = \alpha M_{n-1} = \alpha(\alpha M_{n-2}) = \ldots = \alpha^n M_0 = \alpha^n$$

Also, since the X_i are independent,

$$V_{Z_{n+1}|Z_n=k}Z_{n+1} = V(X_1 + \ldots + X_k) = k\,VX = k\beta$$

where $\beta = VX = G''(1) + \alpha - \alpha^2$. Therefore, from equation 2.22,

$$V_{n+1} = VZ_{n+1} = E_{Z_n}V_{Z_{n+1}|Z_n=Z_n}Z_{n+1} + V_{Z_n}E_{Z_{n+1}|Z_n=Z_n}Z_{n+1}$$

$$= E_{Z_n}(Z_n\beta) + V_{Z_n}(Z_n\alpha) = \beta M_n + \alpha^2 V_n = \beta\alpha^n + \alpha^2 V_n \qquad (4.15)$$

This is a recurrence relation. If $\alpha = 1$, then we easily see that $V_n = n\beta$. If $\alpha \neq 1$, we can solve successively with $n = 0, 1, 2, \ldots$. Alternatively, let us use equation 4.14

$$E_{Z_{n+1}|X=x}Z_{n+1} = x\,EZ_n = xM_n = x\alpha^n$$

$$V_{Z_{n+1}|X=x}Z_{n+1} = x\,VZ_n = xV_n$$

Therefore

$$V_{n+1} = VZ_{n+1} = E_X V_{Z_{n+1}|X=x}Z_{n+1} + V_X E_{Z_{n+1}|X=x}Z_{n+1}$$

$$= E_X(XV_n) + V_X(X\alpha^n) = V_n EX + \alpha^{2n}VX = \alpha^{2n}\beta + \alpha V_n \qquad (4.16)$$

This is another recurrence relation for V_n. If $\alpha \neq 1$, we solve by subtracting (4.15) from (4.16) to obtain

$$\alpha(1-\alpha)V_n = \beta\alpha^n(1-\alpha^n)$$

i.e.

$$V_n = \begin{cases} \beta n & (\alpha = 1) \\ \beta\alpha^{n-1}\left(\dfrac{1-\alpha^n}{1-\alpha}\right) & (\alpha \neq 1) \end{cases}$$

$\square$

Problem 4.16 Show that the population process $\{Z_n : n = 0, 1, 2, \ldots\}$ is a Markov chain, and find its transition matrix. If $Z_0 = 1$, what is the chance that the population will eventually become extinct? What if the process starts with i individuals?

Solution. Since

$$Z_{n+1} = \begin{cases} X_1 + \ldots + X_{Z_n} & (Z_n = 1, 2, \ldots) \\ 0 & (Z_n = 0) \end{cases} \qquad (4.17)$$

and the X_i are independent rvs, each having known pgf $G(s)$, we see that the process is an MC. Let

49

$$p_{ij} = \text{pr}(Z_{n+1} = j \mid Z_n = i)$$

Then clearly

$p_{0j} = \delta_{0j}$ (the Kronecker delta), i.e. state 0 is absorbing

$p_{1j} = \text{pr}(X = j) = p_j,$ say

But what is p_{ij} ($i = 2, 3, 4, \ldots$)? Given $Z_n = i$, from (4.17) and Problem 2.12,

$$P_i(s) = \sum_{j=0}^{\infty} p_{ij} s^j = E_{Z_{n+1} \mid Z_n = i} s^{Z_n} = \{G(s)\}^i$$

so p_{ij} is the coefficient of s^j in $\{G(s)\}^i$.

If $Z_0 = 1$, the probability that the population is extinct on or before the nth generation is $p_{10}^{(n)} = \text{pr}(Z_n = 0 \mid Z_0 = 1) = q_n$ say. Clearly q_n increases as time passes, that is as n increases. We can assume that $0 < p_0 = p_{10} = q_1 \leqslant 1$, since if $p_0 = 0$ no extinction is possible. The sequence $\{q_n : n = 1, 2, \ldots\}$ is therefore bounded above (by 1) and increasing, and so must have a limit q. But by (4.12)

$$q_n = \Pi_n(0) = G\{\Pi_{n-1}(0)\} = G(q_{n-1}) \tag{4.18}$$

Therefore, as $n \to \infty$, limit q satisfies

$$q = G(q) \tag{4.19}$$

We note that, since $G(1) = E_X 1^X = 1$, $q = 1$ is always a solution. There may be another solution and, if there is, it is the one we want. To prove this, let q^* be any root. Then since $G(q)$ is a power series in q with positive coefficients (they are probabilities) it increases in $0 < q < 1$ as q increases, so by (4.18)

$$q_1 = G(0) < G(q^*) = q^* \tag{4.20}$$

and

$$q_2 = G(q_1) < G(q^*) = q^*$$

(since, by (4.20) $q_1 < q^*$, so $G(q_1) < G(q^*)$).

By induction, $q_n < q^*$. Therefore, as $n \to \infty$

$$q = \lim_{n \to \infty} q_n \leqslant q^*$$

and so the chance of extinction, q, is the smallest positive root of $q = G(q)$.

If the process started with i individuals, the probability of extinction is the chance that each of the i lines independently dies out. It is therefore q^i, where q is the smallest positive root of $q = G(q)$. $\qquad \square$

Computationally we have described a simple iterative procedure for solving equation 4.19, namely

$$q_{n+1} = G(q_n), \qquad q_1 = p_0$$

The condition separating the cases $q = 1$ and $q < 1$ is given by observing the slope at $s = 1$ of the function $G(s)$ (see Figure 4.2).

50

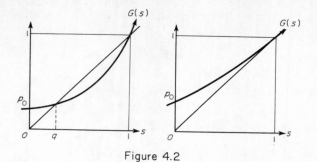

Figure 4.2

The slope at $s = 1$ is $G'(1) = EX = \alpha$, the expected family size; and so

$$q \begin{cases} = 1 \\ < 1 \end{cases} \quad \text{according to whether } \alpha \begin{cases} \leqslant 1 \\ > 1 \end{cases}$$

4.4 Classification of the states of a Markov chain State j is *periodic* with period d if

$$p_{jj}^{(md)} > 0 \quad (m = 1, 2, \ldots), \qquad p_{jj}^{(n)} = 0 \quad (n \neq md)$$

i.e. the particle can return to its initial state j only at times d, $2d$, ... The period d is the greatest common divisor of all n for which $p_{jj}^{(n)} > 0$. If $d = 1$, then state j is called *aperiodic*. Each state of the unrestricted random walk on the integers (Problem 3.1) has period 2 since the particle can only return to it in an even number of steps.

Let rv T_{jj} be the time at which the particle returns to state j for the first time, where $T_{jj} = 1$ if the particle stays in j for a time unit. The state j is *recurrent* if $\mathrm{pr}(T_{jj} < \infty) = 1$ and *transient* if $\mathrm{pr}(T_{jj} < \infty) < 1$.

Let rv T_{ij} be the time for the particle to go from state i to state j for the first time. Then T_{ij} is called the *first passage time* from i to j. (See Problem 3.15.) Let T_{ij} have pgf $F_{ij}(s)$. If $P_{ij}(s) = \sum_{n=0}^{\infty} p_{ij}^{(n)} s^n$, then

$$P_{ij}(s) - \delta_{ij} = F_{ij}(s) P_{ij}(s) \tag{4.21}$$

where δ_{ij} is the Kronecker delta. This is the *renewal equation*.

Problem 4.17 Derive the *renewal equation*.

Solution. Let rv $M_{ij}^{(k)}$ be the time at which the particle starting in state i is in state j for the kth time. Then $M_{ij}^{(1)} = T_{ij}$ and

$$M_{ij}^{(k)} = T_{ij} + T_{jj}^{(1)} + T_{jj}^{(2)} + \ldots + T_{jj}^{(k-1)} \quad (k = 2, 3, \ldots)$$

where each term, by the Markov property, is independently distributed,

51

and, by the time independence of the MC, each $T_{jj}^{(n)}$ is distributed as T_{jj}. Then, if $M_{ij}^{(k)}$ has pgf $G_{ijk}(s)$,

$$G_{ijk}(s) = F_{ij}(s)\{F_{jj}(s)\}^{k-1} = F_{ij}(s)G_{j,j,k-1}(s) \quad (k = 1, 2, 3, \ldots).$$

Now by (2.1)

$$p_{ij}^{(n)} = \mathrm{pr}(M_{ij}^{(1)} = n \quad \text{or} \quad M_{ij}^{(2)} = n \quad \text{or} \ldots)$$
$$= \mathrm{pr}(M_{ij}^{(1)} = n) + \mathrm{pr}(M_{ij}^{(2)} = n) + \ldots .$$

Multiply by s^n, and sum over $n = 1, 2, \ldots$.

$$P_{ij}(s) - p_{ij}^{(0)} = \sum_{n=1}^{\infty} p_{ij}^{(n)} s^n = G_{ij1}(s) + G_{ij2}(s) + G_{ij3}(s) + \ldots \qquad (4.22)$$
$$= F_{ij}(s)(1 + G_{jj1}(s) + G_{jj2}(s) + \ldots)$$
$$= F_{ij}(s)[1 + \{P_{jj}(s) - p_{jj}^{(0)}\}]$$

by setting $i = j$ in (4.22). Then (4.21) follows by noting that $p_{ij}^{(0)} = \delta_{ij}$. $\square$

When $i = j$ and $s = 1$ we have

$$P_{jj}(1) = \{1 - F_{jj}(1)\}^{-1}$$

then, since $\mathrm{pr}(T_{jj} < \infty) = F_{jj}(1)$, the condition $F_{jj}(1) = 1$ is equivalent to $P_{jj}(1) = \infty$, and $F_{jj}(1) < 1$ to $P_{jj}(1) < \infty$. Thus state j is *recurrent* or *transient* according to whether $P_{jj}(1) = \infty$ or $P_{jj}(1) < \infty$.

Problem 4.18 Determine $F_{ij}(s)$ and $P_{ij}(s)$ for the unrestricted random walk of Problem 3.1 for every integer i and j.

Solution. The solution of Problem 3.4 is that

$$P_{00}(s) = u(s), \qquad P_{01}(s) = \{u(s) - 1\}/2qs \qquad (4.23)$$

where $u(s) = (1 - 4pqs^2)^{-\frac{1}{2}}$. By symmetry we can interchange p and q to obtain

$$P_{10}(s) = \{u(s) - 1\}/2ps$$

Starting in state i, the particle cannot be allowed to pass through state 0 if it is reaching 0 for the first time. State 0 can therefore be treated as an absorbing barrier. Then (for $i > 0$) $F_{i0}(s)$ is the pgf for the time to a gambler's ruin if he starts with £i. In Problem 3.11 we saw that

$$F_{i0}(s) = \{F_{10}(s)\}^i \quad (i > 0).$$

By the stationarity of the random walk (Problem 3.5)

$$P_{i+j,j}(s) = P_{i0}(s), \qquad F_{i+j,j}(s) = F_{i0}(s)$$

From equation 4.21,

$$F_{00}(s) = 1 - \{P_{00}(s)\}^{-1} = 1 - \{u(s)\}^{-1}$$

and

$$P_{i0}(s) = F_{i0}(s)P_{00}(s) = \{F_{10}(s)\}^i P_{00}(s) \quad (i = 1, 2, \ldots)$$

Therefore from the case $i = 1$

$$F_{10}(s) = P_{10}(s)\{P_{00}(s)\}^{-1} = [1 - \{u(s)\}^{-1}]/2ps \qquad (4.24)$$

The alternative solution of Problem 3.11 is completed by equation 4.24. Together the displayed equations from (4.23) to (4.24) enable us to determine $F_{ij}(s)$ and $P_{ij}(s)$ for every $i \geqslant j$. Similarly

$$F_{-i,0}(s) = \{F_{-1,0}(s)\}^i$$

where, by symmetry, $F_{-1,0}(s)$ is $F_{10}(s)$ with p and q interchanged, i.e. $[1 - \{u(s)\}^{-1}]/2qs$. Then

$$P_{-i,0}(s) = F_{-i,0}(s)P_{00}(s) = \{F_{-1,0}(s)\}^i P_{00}(s) \quad (i = 1, 2, \ldots)$$

and so we obtain $F_{ij}(s)$ and $P_{ij}(s)$ for every integer i and j. ☐

Problem 4.19 Determine ET_{i0} and VT_{i0} for the unrestricted random walk.

Solution. From $F_{10}(s)$ by equations 2.24 we find that if $p < q$

$$ET_{10} = (q-p)^{-1}, \qquad VT_{10} = 4pq/(q-p)^3$$

Therefore, from equation 3.11

$$ET_{i0} = i\,ET_{10} = i(q-p)^{-1}, \qquad VT_{i0} = i\,VT_{10} = 4pqi/(q-p)^3$$

If $p \geqslant q$, $F_1'(1) = \infty$, $F_1''(1) = \infty$ and so the moments ET_{i0} and VT_{i0} do not exist. ☐

State i is *null-recurrent* if i is recurrent and $ET_{ii} = \infty$; state i is *positive-recurrent* if i is recurrent and $ET_{ii} < \infty$.

State i *leads to* state j (we write: $i \to j$) if for some integer $k \geqslant 0$, $p_{ij}^{(k)} > 0$. The particle then has positive probability of reaching state j from state i. States i and j *communicate* (we write: $i \leftrightarrow j$) if $i \to j$ and $j \to i$. Now $\leftrightarrow$ is an equivalence relation, so the states may be partitioned into equivalence classes, called the *irreducible* classes of the Markov chain. A Markov chain of just one class is called *irreducible*. Clearly, whilst it is possible for a particle to leave an irreducible class to visit another, it can never return, otherwise the two irreducible classes would communicate and be a single class. The random walk with 2 absorbing barriers has 3 classes.

Both periodicity and recurrence/transience are class properties. For an MC with only finitely many states, at least one state must be recurrent, and every recurrent state must be positive recurrent. The reader should be able to argue why this is so.

Kolmogorov's theorem is that if an MC is irreducible and aperiodic, then there is a π_j such that

$$p_{ij}^{(n)} \to \pi_j \quad \text{as} \quad n \to \infty$$

The $\{\pi_j\}$ is the equilibrium distribution, which by this theorem exists, and which we have seen satisfies equation 4.4:

$$\pi' = \pi'\mathbf{P}$$

If an MC has an equilibrium distribution it is called *ergodic*. It then forms a single irreducible class, and every state is positive recurrent and aperiodic.

Problem 4.20   Show that the unrestricted random walk with $p = q = \frac{1}{2}$ is null-recurrent.

Solution. $\qquad\qquad P_{ii}(s) = P_{00}(s) = (1-s^2)^{-\frac{1}{2}}$

Therefore

$$P_{ii}(1) = \infty$$

so the random walk is recurrent.

$$F_{ii}(s) = 1 - \{P_{ii}(s)\}^{-1} = 1 - (1-s^2)^{\frac{1}{2}}$$

so

$$\mathrm{E}T_{ii} = F'_{ii}(1) = \lim_{s \to 1} s(1-s^2)^{-\frac{1}{2}} = \infty$$

therefore the random walk is null-recurrent. $\qquad\qquad\qquad\qquad$ $\square$

Problem 4.21   *A simple storage model.* The following is a simple model of storage for a disposable or edible commodity, such as razor blades or bottles of wine. At each time instant an item may be consumed. When stocks run out, j items ($j = 0, 1, 2, \ldots$) are purchased with probability r_j. Consider an irreducible MC with transition probabilities

$$\begin{aligned}
p_{0j} &= r_j & (j &= 0, 1, 2, \ldots) \\
p_{ii} &= p & (i &= 1, 2, \ldots) \\
p_{i,i-1} &= q = 1-p & (i &= 1, 2, \ldots)
\end{aligned}$$

Find the pgf $F_{i0}(s)$ for the first passage time T_{i0} from state i to state 0. Show that the MC is positive or null-recurrent according to whether the mean of the distribution $\{r_j\}$ is finite or infinite.

Solution. In state i (>0) the next step is to $i-1$ with probability q or no change with probability p. Now

$$T_{i0} = T_{i,i-1} + T_{i-1,i-2} + \ldots + T_{10}$$

where each component is independently distributed like T_{10}. We consider a decomposition based on the first step, X. Given $X = -1$, $T_{10} = 1$ and $\mathrm{E}_{T_{10}|X=-1} s^{T_{10}} = s^1 = s$; and given $X = 0$, $T_{10} = 1 + T'_{10}$ where T'_{10} is distributed like T_{10}, so

$$\mathrm{E}_{T_{10}|X=0} \, s^{T_{10}} = \mathrm{E}_{T_{10}} s^{1+T_{10}} = sF_{10}(s)$$

Therefore

54

$$F_{10}(s) = \mathrm{E}s^{T_{10}} = \mathrm{E}_X \, \mathrm{E}_{T|X=X} \, s^{T_{10}}$$
$$= \mathrm{pr}(X = -1)s + \mathrm{pr}(X = 0)sF_{10}(s) = qs + psF_{10}(s)$$

Therefore

$$F_{10}(s) = qs/(1-ps)$$

Therefore

$$F_{io}(s) = \{F_{10}(s)\}^i = \{qs/(1-ps)\}^i$$

The chain is given to be irreducible. (The sequence $\{r_j\}$ must therefore have an infinite number of nonzero elements.) To study recurrence we need therefore investigate only one state. It is convenient to examine state 0. Given that $X = 0$, then $T_{00} = 1$; and given that $X = j$, then $T_{00} = 1 + T_{j0}$. Therefore

$$\mathrm{E}_{T_{00}|X=j} \, s^{T_{00}} = \mathrm{E}_{T_{j0}} \, s^{1 + T_{j0}} = s\{F_{10}(s)\}^j$$

Therefore

$$F_{00}(s) = \mathrm{E}_X \, \mathrm{E}_{T_{00}|X=X} \, s^{T_{00}} = r_0 s + s \sum_{j=1}^{\infty} r_j \{F_{10}(s)\}^j = s \sum_{j=0}^{\infty} \left(\frac{qs}{1-ps}\right)^j r_j$$

$$= sR\{qs/(1-ps)\}, \quad \text{where} \quad R(s) = \sum_{j=0}^{\infty} r_j s^j$$

Therefore

$$F_{00}(1) = R(1) = 1 \quad \text{since } \{r_j\} \text{ is a distribution}$$

State 0 is therefore recurrent, and so the MC is recurrent.

Further, $F'_{00}(1) = 1 + \dfrac{1}{q} R'(1)$, where $R'(1)$ is the mean of the distribution $\{r_j\}$. $F'_{00}(1)$ is infinite or finite according to whether $R'(1)$ is infinite or finite. This is the condition for state 0 (and so also the MC) to be null or positive recurrent. $\qquad\square$

Problem 4.22   Each morning, records of the previous day's business arrive at the accounts office to be entered in the ledgers. The office on any day is capable of writing up k days' records with probability p_k $(k = 0, 1, 2, \ldots)$. Show that, if the office staff work diligently, Z_n, the number of days' records at the start of day n waiting to be written up, forms a Markov chain, and find its transition matrix.

Show that the trial solution $\pi_j = (1-\lambda)\lambda^{j-1}$ $(j = 1, 2, \ldots)$ satisfies the equations for the equilibrium distribution. What in this equilibrium situation is the probability that the previous day's accounts will be dealt with immediately on arrival at the office?

Solution. Let X_n be the number of days' records actually dealt with on day n. Then the number waiting on day $n+1$ is the number waiting on day n, plus that for day n, less those dealt with on day n, i.e.

$$Z_{n+1} = Z_n + 1 - X_n$$

and this depends only on Z_n and an rv X_n which depends only on Z_n, so the process is an MC. Now X_n is the number capable of being dealt with if at least that number is waiting, otherwise X_n is the number waiting. Therefore

$$\text{pr}(X_n = j \,|\, Z_n = i) = \begin{cases} p_j & (j = 0, 1, \ldots, i-1) \\ \sum_{k=i}^{\infty} p_k = P_i \text{ say} & (j = i) \\ 0 & (\text{otherwise}) \end{cases}$$

Therefore

$$p_{ij} = \text{pr}(Z_{n+1} = j \,|\, Z_n = i) = \text{pr}(Z_n + 1 - X_n = j \,|\, Z_n = i)$$

$$= \text{pr}(X_n = i+1-j \,|\, Z_n = i) = \begin{cases} P_i & (i+1-j = i; \text{ i.e. } j = 1) \\ p_{i+1-j} & (i+1-j = 0, 1, \ldots, i-1; \\ & \quad \text{i.e. } j = 2, 3, \ldots, i+1) \\ 0 & (\text{otherwise}) \end{cases}$$

i.e. the transition matrix is

$$
\begin{array}{c c}
 & \begin{array}{ccccc} 1 & 2 & 3 & 4 & 5 \cdots \end{array} \\
\mathbf{P} = \begin{array}{c} 1 \\ 2 \\ 3 \\ \vdots \end{array} & \begin{pmatrix} P_1 & p_0 & 0 & 0 & 0 & \cdots \\ P_2 & p_1 & p_0 & 0 & 0 & \cdots \\ P_3 & p_2 & p_1 & p_0 & 0 & \cdots \\ \vdots & \vdots & \vdots & \vdots & \vdots & \end{pmatrix}
\end{array}
$$

The equilibrium equations, $\boldsymbol{\pi}' = \boldsymbol{\pi}'\mathbf{P}$, are

$$\pi_1 = \pi_1 P_1 + \pi_2 P_2 + \pi_3 P_3 + \cdots$$
$$\pi_{k+1} = \pi_k p_0 + \pi_{k+1} p_1 + \pi_{k+2} p_2 + \cdots \qquad (k = 1, 2, \ldots)$$

Using the trial solution: $\pi_j = (1-\lambda)\lambda^{j-1}$, we find that λ must satisfy

$$\lambda = G(\lambda) = \sum_{k=0}^{\infty} p_k \lambda^k$$

where $G(s)$ is a known pgf. This equation emerged in Problem 4.16 about the discrete branching process. We saw there that if $G'(1) \leqslant 1$ then the equation has just one root, $\lambda = 1$. Then $\pi_j = 0$ and does not form a distribution. For equilibrium, therefore, we must have $G'(1) > 1$, and take λ to be the smaller root, λ_0, of $\lambda = G(\lambda)$.

56

The probability of the $(n-1)$th day's business being entered into the ledgers first thing on day n is

$$\mathrm{pr}(Z_{n-1} = 1, \quad X_n \neq 0) \rightarrow \pi_1(1-p_0) = (1-\lambda_0)(1-p_0) \quad \text{as} \quad n \rightarrow \infty$$

□

Problem 4.23 Consider the *library loan process* of Problems 1.5 and 4.5. If $F(t)$ has a finite mean, show that the MC is irreducible, aperiodic and positive recurrent. Find its equilibrium distribution.

Solution. The MC is irreducible since, for each (i,j), $k = j+1$ is such that $p_{ij}^{(k)} > 0$. The possible path from i to j in $j+1$ steps is i to 0 on the first step, from 0 to 1 on the second, then 1 to 2, and so on, ending on the $(j+1)$th step with $j-1$ to j;

$$p_{ij}^{(j+1)} \geqslant p_{i0} \, p_{01} \, p_{12} \cdots p_{j-1,j} > 0$$

Aperiodicity and recurrence are class properties so we consider only the one state, 0, of the irreducible chain. Since $p_{00}^{(1)} = F(1) > 0$, the MC is aperiodic. State 0 is recurrent if $\mathrm{pr}([T+1] < \infty) = 1$, where $[T+1]$ is the number of weeks the book is on loan, i.e. the smallest integer not smaller than T, and is the first return time to state 0. Now $\mathrm{pr}([T+1] < \infty) \geqslant \mathrm{pr}(T+1 < \infty) = F(\infty) = 1$, so the MC is recurrent. Now since $\mathrm{E}[T+1] \leqslant \mathrm{E}(T+1) = \mathrm{E}T+1$, and $\mathrm{E}T < \infty$, we have that $\mathrm{E}[T+1] < \infty$, so the MC is positive recurrent.

An irreducible, aperiodic, positive recurrent MC is ergodic and has an equilibrium distribution, $\boldsymbol{\pi}'$, given by $\boldsymbol{\pi}' = \boldsymbol{\pi}'\mathbf{P}$,

$$\pi_0 = \pi_0 F(1) + \pi_1 \frac{F(2)-F(1)}{1-F(1)} + \pi_2 \frac{F(3)-F(2)}{1-F(2)} + \cdots$$

$$\pi_{j+1} = \pi_j \frac{1-F(j+1)}{1-F(j)} \quad (j = 0,1,2,\ldots)$$

$$= \pi_{j-1} \left\{ \frac{1-F(j)}{1-F(j-1)} \right\} \left\{ \frac{1-F(j+1)}{1-F(j)} \right\} = \pi_{j-1} \frac{1-F(j+1)}{1-F(j-1)}$$

$$= \cdots = \pi_0 \{1-F(j+1)\}$$

Therefore

$$\pi_j = \pi_0 \{1-F(j)\} \quad (j = 0,1,2,\ldots)$$

Since

$$1 = \sum_{j=0}^{\infty} \pi_j = \pi_0 \sum_{j=0}^{\infty} \{1-F(j)\},$$

$$\pi_j = \frac{1-F(j)}{\displaystyle\sum_{k=0}^{\infty} \{1-F(k)\}}$$

□

We can easily show that $\sum_{k=0}^{\infty} \{1 - F(k)\} = E[T+1]$.

Problem 4.24   *Achilles and the tortoise.* Zeno (495–435BC) reported on a race between Achilles and a tortoise. Suppose that the tortoise is given w time units start. Suppose also that during each time unit it runs a distance of a yard or else it stays where it is according to an independent Bernoulli trial with probability of moving θ ($0 < \theta < 1$), and that Achilles runs at a steady rate of one yard each time unit.

During the initial w time units the tortoise will run X_1 yards to position $Z_1 = X_1$. While Achilles is reaching Z_1, the tortoise will run on a further X_2 yards to position $Z_2 = X_1 + X_2$. In general while Achilles is running from Z_{n-1} to Z_n, the tortoise is running a further X_{n+1} yards to $Z_{n+1} = Z_n + X_{n+1}$.

Show that $\{X_n : n = 1, 2, \ldots\}$ is a Markov chain, and that $EX_n = w\theta^n$; hence find EZ_n and the mean of $Z = \lim_{n \to \infty} Z_n$, the position of the tortoise when Achilles catches it up.

Determine the distribution of Z directly.

Solution. X_{n+1} depends only on X_n (it is as though the race starts again with the tortoise having X_n time units start), so $\{X_n\}$ is an MC. Clearly 0 is an absorbing state, when Achilles catches up with the tortoise. Now X_1 is Bin(w, θ) and $X_{n+1} | X_n = k$ is Bin(k, θ). Therefore

$$M_{n+1} = EX_{n+1} = E_{X_n} E_{X_{n+1}|X_n=x_n} X_{n+1} = E_{X_n}(X_n \theta) = \theta M_n$$

Therefore

$$M_n = \theta M_{n-1} = \theta^2 M_{n-2} = \ldots = \theta^{n-1} M_1 = \theta^{n-1}(w\theta) = w\theta^n$$

$$(\to 0 \quad \text{as} \quad n \to \infty).$$

$$EZ_n = E(X_1 + \ldots + X_n) = \sum_{k=1}^{n} M_k = \frac{w\theta}{1-\theta}(1 - \theta^n)$$

$$\left(\to \frac{w\theta}{1-\theta} \quad \text{as} \quad n \to \infty \right).$$

Directly: the tortoise runs a distance Z before Achilles catches up with it, where Z is the number of successes before the wth failure in a sequence of independent Bernoulli trials with probability of success θ; therefore Z is negative binomial, NB($w, 1 - \theta$). $\square$

EXERCISES

1.   *Nuclear chain reactions.* Consider a population of neutrons which are being bombarded by other particles. The neutrons are inactive unless

directly hit by a particle. By fission the particle is then broken into a fixed number, m, of the neutrons, and energy is released. Under a steady stream of bombarding particles each neutron independently in each short unit time interval has a small probability θ of receiving a direct hit. If the number of neutrons initially is mi_0, show that the number present at the nth unit time point is a Markov chain. What is its transition matrix?

2. By defining the sequence $\{X_j : j = 0, 1, 2, \ldots\}$ of Bernoulli rvs, where $X_j = 1$ if $Z_j = i_j$ and $X_j = 0$ otherwise, use the result of Problem 4.6 to establish equation 4.1.

3. *The simple queue model.* Show directly from equation 4.10 that $\Pi_n(s) = Es^{Z_n}$ satisfies recurrence relation

$$s\,\Pi_{n+1}(s) = \{(s-1)\mathrm{pr}(Z_n = 0) + \Pi_n(s)\}P(s) \qquad (4.25)$$

where $P(s)$ is the pgf for X.

If

$$\Pi_n(s) \to \Pi(s) = \sum_{k=0}^{\infty} \pi_k s^k \quad \text{as } n \to \infty,$$

show directly from $EZ_{n+1} = EZ_n - E\Delta_n + EX_n$ that $\pi_0 = 1 - \rho$, where $\rho = EX$. By letting $n \to \infty$ in equation 4.25 find $\Pi(s)$.

4. *A single-server queue with batch arrivals.* Let us call the nth customer served C_n. Let B_n be the number of customers in the first batch to arrive after the departure of C_n, and A_n be the total number of customers who arrive while C_n is being served. If Z_n is the size of the queue at the departure of C_n, show that

$$Z_{n+1} = \begin{cases} Z_n - 1 + A_{n+1} & (Z_n = 1, 2, \ldots) \\ B_n - 1 + A_{n+1} & (Z_n = 0) \end{cases}$$

Suppose that when $Z_n = 0$, B_n is independent of A_{n+1}, the B_n have pgf $B(s)$ and the A_n have pgf $A(s)$. Use the method of Exercise 3 to show that $\Pi_n(s)$, the pgf for Z_n, satisfies

$$s\,\Pi_{n+1}(s) = [\{B(s) - 1\}\mathrm{pr}(Z_n = 0) + \Pi_n(s)]A(s)$$

Deduce the form of the limiting pgf.

5. Consider the 2-state Markov chain $\{X_n : n = 0, 1, 2, \ldots\}$ of Problem 4.9. Show that the process $\{Y_n : n = 0, 1, 2, \ldots\}$, where

$$Y_n = \begin{cases} 0 & \text{if } (X_{2n}, X_{2n+1}) = (0, 1) \\ 1 & \text{if } (X_{2n}, X_{2n+1}) = (1, 0) \\ 2 & \text{if } (X_{2n}, X_{2n+1}) = (0, 0) \\ 3 & \text{if } (X_{2n}, X_{2n+1}) = (1, 1) \end{cases}$$

is an MC, and find its transition matrix. Define the process $\{Z_k : k = 0, 1, 2, \ldots\}$, where Z_k is the sequence constructed by deleting values 2 and 3 from the sequence $\{Y_n\}$. Show that $\{Z_k\}$ is a 2-state MC with transition matrix $p_{00} = p_{11} = \lambda$, $p_{01} = p_{10} = 1-\lambda$, where $\lambda = (3-\alpha-\beta)^{-1}$.

6. *A branching process.* Suppose that every individual at each time $n = 0, 1, 2, \ldots$ becomes a family, where the family sizes are independently distributed with pgf $G(s)$. During each unit time interval $(n, n+1)$ immigrants arrive in numbers which are independently distributed with pgf $H(s)$. Show that $\Pi_n(s)$, the pgf for the population size just after the nth generation, satisfies

$$\Pi_{n+1}(s) = H\{G(s)\}\Pi_n\{G(s)\}$$

7. *A branching process.* For the discrete branching process of Problem 4.14, let rv $Y_k = Z_1 + \ldots + Z_k$ be the total number of descendants in the first k generations. By a decomposition based on Z_1, the number in the first generation, show that $H_k(s)$, the pgf for Y_k satisfies recurrence relation

$$H_k(s) = G\{H_{k-1}(s)\}$$

Deduce a formula for EY_k in terms of EY_{k-1} and the mean family size EZ_1, and use it to find EY_k.

8. Find the classes formed by the states of the Markov chains with the following transition matrices. Describe the classes as transient, positive-recurrent or null-recurrent.

(i) $p_{02} = 1$, $\quad p_{11} = 1$, $\quad p_{i,i-1} = p_{i,i+1} = \frac{1}{2}$ $\quad (i = 2, 3, \ldots)$,
$$p_{ij} = 0 \quad \text{(otherwise)}.$$

(ii) $\begin{pmatrix} \frac{1}{2} & 0 & \frac{1}{2} & 0 \\ 0 & \frac{1}{2} & 0 & \frac{1}{2} \\ \frac{1}{2} & 0 & \frac{1}{2} & 0 \\ 0 & \frac{1}{2} & 0 & \frac{1}{2} \end{pmatrix}$, (iii) $\begin{pmatrix} \frac{1}{2} & \frac{1}{2} & 0 & 0 & 0 & 0 \\ \frac{1}{2} & \frac{1}{2} & 0 & 0 & 0 & 0 \\ 0 & 0 & \frac{1}{2} & \frac{1}{2} & 0 & 0 \\ 0 & 0 & \frac{1}{2} & \frac{1}{2} & 0 & 0 \\ \frac{1}{6} & \frac{1}{6} & \frac{1}{6} & \frac{1}{6} & \frac{1}{6} & \frac{1}{6} \\ \frac{1}{6} & \frac{1}{6} & \frac{1}{6} & \frac{1}{6} & \frac{1}{6} & \frac{1}{6} \end{pmatrix}$

9. *A random walk with a single impenetrable barrier.* Show that the Markov chain with states $\{0, 1, 2, \ldots\}$ and having transition probabilities

$$p_{00} = q_0, \qquad p_{01} = p_0$$
$$p_{i,i-1} = q_i, \qquad p_{i,i+1} = p_i \quad (i = 1, 2, 3, \ldots)$$
$$p_{ij} = 0 \quad \text{(otherwise)}$$

where $p_i + q_i = 1$ $(i = 0, 1, 2, \ldots)$, has an equilibrium distribution if and only if the series Σr_k converges, where

$$r_k = (p_0 p_1 \cdots p_k)/(q_1 q_2 \cdots q_{k+1})$$

10. *The dam storage model.* Consider the dam storage model of Problem 1.6. Suppose that the daily inputs $\{Y_n\}$ are independent, identically distributed rvs with pgf $G(s) = \sum_{k=0}^{\infty} g_k s^k$. Show that $\{Z_n\}$, where Z_n is the content after the unit release on day n, is a Markov chain, and find its transition matrix.

If $(\pi_0, \pi_1, \ldots, \pi_{w-1})$ is the equilibrium distribution, prove that $v_k = \pi_k/\pi_0$ $(k = 0, 1, 2, \ldots, w-2)$ does not depend on w, and that $\sum_{k=0}^{\infty} v_k s^k = G(0)(1-s)/\{G(s)-s\}$. If the inputs have a geometric distribution, what is this equilibrium distribution?

11. *Achilles and the tortoise.* For Problem 4.24, show that

$$\mathrm{V}X_n = w\theta^n(1-\theta^n), \qquad \mathrm{cov}(X_n, X_{n+m}) = w\theta^{n+m}(1-\theta^n).$$

61

Chapter 5

The Poisson Process

We now consider stochastic processes in which changes of state occur at random time points. First we define the *Poisson process* $\{N_{0t} : t \in [0, \infty)\}$, which gives the times of these jumps. Let rv $N_{t\tau}$ be the number of point events which occur in time interval $(t, \tau]$. If the stochastic process $\{N_{0t} : t \in [0, \infty)\}$ is

(i) time independent, i.e. for each k, $\mathrm{pr}(N_{t.t+\tau} = k)$ depends only on τ (5.1)

(ii) has independent increments, and is   (5.2)

(iii) *orderly*, i.e. $\mathrm{pr}(N_{t,t+\tau} \geqslant 2) = o(\tau)$ as $\tau \to 0$
where, if $A(\tau) = o(\tau)$ as $\tau \to 0$, then $A(\tau)/\tau \to 0$ as $\tau \to 0$ (5.3)

then the process is a *Poisson process*.

Problem 5.1 Show that $\{N_{0t}\}$ is a Poisson process if, for a positive constant λ,

(i)
$$\mathrm{pr}(N_{t,t+\Delta} = 0) = 1 - \lambda\Delta + o(\Delta)$$
$$\mathrm{pr}(N_{t,t+\Delta} = 1) = \lambda\Delta + o(\Delta)$$
$$\mathrm{pr}(N_{t,t+\Delta} \geqslant 2) = o(\Delta)$$

and

(ii) $N_{t,t+\Delta}$ is independent of N_{0t} for all t and Δ.

Solution. By (ii) $\{N_{0t}\}$ has independent increments. Since the probabilities in (i) do not depend on t, $\{N_{0t}\}$ is time independent. We are given that $\{N_{0t}\}$ is orderly; so $\{N_{0t}\}$ is a Poisson process. $\square$

Problem 5.2 Prove that, for fixed t, N_{0t} is $\mathscr{P}(\lambda t)$.

Solution. We shall abbreviate N_{0t} to N_t here and in the following problems. Let $\Pi_t(s) = \mathrm{E}s^{N_t}$, then
$$\Pi_{t+\Delta}(s) = \mathrm{E}s^{N_t + \Delta} = \mathrm{E}s^{N_t + (N_{t+\Delta} - N_t)}$$
By (5.2), N_t and $N_{t+\Delta} - N_t$ are independent and, by (5.1), $N_{t+\Delta} - N_t$ is distributed as $N_\Delta - N_0 = N_\Delta$ (since $N_0 = 0$). Therefore
$$\Pi_{t+\Delta}(s) = \Pi_t(s)\mathrm{E}s^{N_\Delta} = \Pi_t(s)\left\{\sum_{k=0}^{\infty} \mathrm{pr}(N_\Delta = k)s^k\right\}$$
$$= \Pi_t(s)\{(1 - \lambda\Delta)s^0 + \lambda\Delta s^1 + o(\Delta)\} \quad \text{by condition (i) of Problem 5.1}$$
Therefore
$$\frac{\Pi_{t+\Delta}(s) - \Pi_t(s)}{\Delta} = -\lambda(1 - s)\Pi_t(s) + \frac{o(\Delta)}{\Delta}$$

Let $\Delta \to 0$, then
$$\frac{d\Pi_t(s)}{dt} = -\lambda(1-s)\Pi_t(s)$$
Therefore
$$\Pi_t(s) = e^{-\lambda t(1-s)}$$
the pgf for a $\mathscr{P}(\lambda t)$ rv, where we have used $\Pi_0(s) = \mathrm{E}s^{N_0} = \mathrm{E}s^0 = 1$. ☐

Problem 5.3 *The unrestricted random walk in continuous time.* Suppose that a particle starts at the origin and makes a sequence of independent steps: $+1$ with probability p, -1 with probability $q = 1-p$ at time instants $T_1, T_2, \ldots$, which occur as a Poisson process having rate parameter λ (see Figure 5.1).

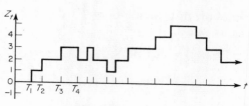

Figure 5.1

What is the distribution of Z_t, the position of the particle at time t, $t \in [0, \infty)$?

Solution. Essentially we have the bivariate process $\{Z_t, N_t : t \in [0, \infty)\}$. The kth step is a rv
$$X_k = \begin{cases} 1 & \text{with probability } p \\ -1 & \text{with probability } q \end{cases}$$
which has pgf $ps + qs^{-1}$. Then
$$Z_t = X_1 + \ldots + X_{N_t}, \qquad Z_t = 0 \quad (\text{if } N_t = 0)$$
so, by Problem 2.14,
$$G_t(s) = \mathrm{E}_{Z_t} s^{Z_t} = \mathrm{E}_{N_t}(ps + qs^{-1})^{N_t} = \exp\{-\lambda t(1 - ps - qs^{-1})\}$$ ☐

Problem 5.4 Determine $\mathrm{E}Z_t$, $\mathrm{V}Z_t$.

Solution. By equations 3.4,
$$\mathrm{E}_{Z_t|N_t=k} Z_t = k(p-q), \qquad \mathrm{V}_{Z_t|N_t=k} Z_t = 4kpq$$
Therefore, by equation 2.20,
$$\mathrm{E}_{Z_t} Z_t = \mathrm{E}_{N_t} \mathrm{E}_{Z_t|N_t=N_t} Z_t = (p-q)\mathrm{E}_{N_t} N_t = (p-q)\lambda t;$$
and by equation 2.22

63

F

$$\begin{aligned}
V_{Z_t} Z_t &= E_{N_t} V_{Z_t|N_t=N_t} Z_t + V_{N_t} E_{Z_t|N_t=N_t} Z_t \\
&= 4pq\, E_{N_t} N_t + V_{N_t}\{(p-q)N_t\} \\
&= 4pq\lambda t + (p-q)^2 \lambda t = \lambda t \qquad \square
\end{aligned}$$

Alternatively, we could have applied equation 2.24 to $G_t(s)$.

Problem 5.5 Find the distribution of rv T, the time to the first event of a Poisson process of rate λ.

Solution. $\mathrm{pr}(T > t) = \mathrm{pr}$ (the first event occurs later than time t)
$$= \mathrm{pr}(N_{0t} = 0) = e^{-\lambda t}$$

Therefore, $\mathrm{pr}(T \leqslant t) = 1 - e^{-\lambda t}$, which, by equation 2.2, is the distribution function of an $\mathscr{E}(\lambda)$ rv. $\qquad \square$

Problem 5.6 Find the distribution of rv T^*, the time between events of a Poisson process of rate λ.

Solution. $\mathrm{pr}(T^* > t) = \lim\limits_{\Delta \to 0} \mathrm{pr}(N_{\tau+\Delta,\tau+\Delta+t} = 0 \,|\, N_{\tau,\tau+\Delta} = 1)$
$$= \lim\limits_{\Delta \to 0} \mathrm{pr}(N_{\tau+\Delta,\tau+\Delta+t} = 0)$$

(since $N_{\tau,\tau+\Delta}$ and $N_{\tau+\Delta,\tau+\Delta+t}$ are independent)
$$= \mathrm{pr}(N_{0t} = 0)$$

(by time independence), and so by Problem 5.5, T^* is distributed as T and is $\mathscr{E}(\lambda)$. $\qquad \square$

Problem 5.7 *First passage times for the unrestricted random walk.* Suppose $p < q$. Find the distribution of rv T_{k0}, the first passage time from state k to state 0 (see Figure 5.2).

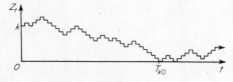

Figure 5.2

Solution. As in the discrete time case of Problem 3.11, a first passage from state k to state 0 implies successive first passages from k to $k-1$, from $k-1$ to $k-2$, ..., from 1 to 0, i.e.
$$T_{k0} = T_{k,k-1} + T_{k-1,k-2} + \ldots + T_{10}$$

where each $T_{j,j-1}$ is independently distributed as T_{10}. The characteristic function $\phi_{k0}(\theta)$ for T_{k0} is therefore $\{\phi_{10}(\theta)\}^k$. We condition on the first step which occurs at a random time T, which by Problem 5.5, is an $\mathscr{E}(\lambda)$ rv.

$$T_{10} = \begin{cases} T+T_{00} = T & \text{with probability } q \\ T+T_{20} & \text{with probability } p \end{cases}$$

depending on whether the first jump, X_1, was -1 or $+1$. Therefore

$$\phi_{10}(\theta) = E_{T_{10}}e^{i\theta T_{10}} = E_{X_1}E_{T_{10}|X_1=X_1}\,e^{i\theta T_{10}} = qEe^{i\theta T}+pEe^{i\theta(T+T_{20})}$$
$$= q\psi(\theta)+p\psi(\theta)Ee^{i\theta T_{20}}$$
$$= \psi(\theta)\{q+p\phi_{20}(\theta)\} = \psi(\theta)[q+p\{\phi_{10}(\theta)\}^2]$$

where $\psi(\theta) = \lambda/(\lambda-i\theta)$ is, by Exercise 14 of Chapter 2, the cf for T. We solve this quadratic equation in ϕ_{10}, keeping θ constant; and since $\phi_{10}(0) = 1$ (for $p < q$)

$$\phi_{10}(\theta) = \{1-\sqrt{(1-4pq\psi^2)}\}/2p\psi$$

where $\psi = \psi(\theta)$. $\qquad\qquad\qquad\qquad\qquad\qquad\qquad\qquad\qquad\qquad\qquad\square$

Problem 5.8 We recall from Problem 4.18 that for the discrete time random walk having $p \leqslant q$, the first passage time pgf from state 1 to state 0 was

$$F_{10}(s) = \{1-\sqrt{(1-4pqs^2)}\}/2ps$$

Why might we have expected the relationship $\phi_{10}(\theta) = F_{10}(\psi(\theta))$?

Solution. In discrete time the first step occurs after unit time, so $Es^T = Es^1 = s$; in continuous time $Ee^{i\theta T} = \psi(\theta)$. $\qquad\qquad\qquad\square$

Problem 5.9 Events occur as a Poisson process of rate λ. The number of events in $(0, X)$, where X is an rv, is an rv Y. Find the pgf for Y in terms of the cf for X.

Solution. $E_{Y|X=t}s^Y = e^{-\lambda t(1-s)}$. Therefore

$$G_Y(s) = E_Y s^Y = E_X E_{Y|X=x}s^Y = E_X e^{-\lambda X(1-s)} = E_X \exp[i\{i\lambda(1-s)\}X]$$
$$= \phi_X\{i\lambda(1-s)\} \qquad\qquad\qquad\qquad\qquad\qquad\qquad\square$$

Problem 5.10 Two independent Poisson processes have rates λ and v respectively. Find the distribution of rv Y, the number of events in the first process which occur before the first event of the second process.

Solution. The time X to the first event of the second process has cf $\phi_X(\theta) = v/(v-i\theta)$. Therefore, by Problem 5.9,

$$G_Y(s) = \phi_X\{i\lambda(1-s)\} = \frac{v}{v+\lambda(1-s)} = \frac{1-\lambda/(\lambda+v)}{1-\lambda s/(\lambda+v)}$$
$$= \frac{v/(\lambda+v)}{1-s\{1-v/(\lambda+v)\}}$$

65

which is the pgf for a $\mathscr{G}(v/(\lambda+v))$ rv (Exercise 10 of Chapter 2).

EXERCISES

1. Customers arrive in a Poisson process at the rate of one per minute at a newspaper seller's stand to buy the evening paper. If the seller has just 2 copies left and will not receive a supply of the next edition for 5 minutes, what is the distribution of the number of his disappointed customers?

2. If $\{N_{0t}\}$ is a Poisson process having rate parameter λ then, since the process has independent increments, the numbers of events occurring in non-overlapping time intervals are independent and so, by equation 2.18 and Problem 2.7, have zero covariance. Also $VN_{0t} = \lambda t$. Use these results to show that the process $\{N_{t,t+\tau}: t \in [0, \infty), \tau \text{ fixed}\}$ has covariance function

$$g(s, t) = \text{cov}(N_{s,s+\tau}, N_{t,t+\tau}) = \begin{cases} \lambda(\tau - |t-s|) & (|t-s| \leqslant \tau) \\ 0 & (|t-s| > \tau). \end{cases}$$

3. *Insurance claims.* Claims are made on an insurance company at times $T_1, T_2, \ldots$, where $0 < T_1 < T_2 < \ldots$, which are events of a Poisson process having rate parameter λ. If the claim at time T_n is amount X_n, show that the characteristic function for Z_t, the total amount claimed in $(0, t)$, is

$$\exp[-\lambda t\{1 - \phi(\theta)\}]$$

where the X_n are independent rvs having cf $\phi(\theta)$.

4. *Stock control.* Orders for a certain item are placed according to a Poisson process having rate parameter λ. The quantities ordered are independent $\mathscr{E}(v)$ rvs. What is the cf for the total demand over an interval of length t?

Chapter 6

Markov Chains with Continuous Time Parameters

6.1 The theory Here we consider a Markov process $\{Z_t : t \in [0, \infty)\}$ having a discrete state space S, and time-independent transition probabilities

$$p_{ij}(t) = \text{pr}(Z_{\tau+t} = j \mid Z_\tau = i) \quad (i, j \in S; \ t, \tau \in [0, \infty))$$

The transition matrix is $\mathbf{P}(t) = (p_{ij}(t)) \quad (i, j \in S)$

(i) For any $t \in [0, \infty)$, $p_{ij}(t) \geqslant 0$, $\sum_{j \in S} p_{ij}(t) = 1$,

i.e. $\mathbf{P}(t)$ is a stochastic matrix.

(ii) A *continuity condition*. As $t \to 0$, $p_{ii}(t) \to 1$; then by (i) $p_{ij}(t) \to 0$ as $t \to 0$ for $i \neq j$; therefore $p_{ij}(t) \to \delta_{ij}$,

i.e. $\mathbf{P}(t) \to \mathbf{I}$ as $t \to 0$.

(iii) The *Chapman–Kolmogorov equation* holds, i.e.

$$\mathbf{P}(u+v) = \mathbf{P}(u)\mathbf{P}(v) \quad (u, v \in [0, \infty)) \tag{6.1}$$

If S is finite, then the unique solution of equation 6.1 is

$$\mathbf{P}(u) = e^{u\mathbf{Q}} = \sum_{n=0}^{\infty} \frac{(u\mathbf{Q})^n}{n!} \tag{6.2}$$

where $\mathbf{Q}$ is a constant matrix. Given $\mathbf{Q}$ we can find $\mathbf{P}(t)$, and given $\mathbf{P}(t)$ we can find $\mathbf{Q}$. Thus $\mathbf{Q}$ can be used to 'represent' the process.

If a remainder term $A(t) = O(t)$ as $t \to 0$, then $|A(t)/t| < c$, a positive constant, as $t \to 0$. Then from equation 6.2, as $t \to 0$

$$\mathbf{P}(t) = \mathbf{I} + t\mathbf{Q} + O(t^2)$$

i.e.
$$p_{ij}(t) = \delta_{ij} + t q_{ij} + O(t^2)$$

so

$$q_{ij} = \lim_{t \to 0} \frac{p_{ij}(t) - \delta_{ij}}{t} = \frac{d}{dt} \{p_{ij}(t)\} \bigg|_{t=0} = p'_{ij}(0) \quad \text{say} \tag{6.3}$$

since $\delta_{ij} = p_{ij}(0)$ (by (ii)). If $A(t) \sim ct$ as $t \to 0$, then $A(t)/t \to c$ as $t \to 0$. Therefore, for $i \neq j$, $p_{ij}(t) \sim q_{ij}t$ as $t \to 0$. Thus $q_{ij}t$ is the probability of a jump from i to j in short time interval t; q_{ij} is termed the *transition rate* from i to j, and $\mathbf{Q}$ is called the *matrix of transition rates*. From equation 6.3 we can show that if $i \neq j$ then $q_{ij} \geqslant 0$ and that $q_{ii} \leqslant 0$. We therefore set $q_i = -q_{ii} \geqslant 0$.

Problem 6.1 Let rv T_i be the time spent in state i before a jump from it. Prove that T_i is $\mathscr{E}(q_i)$.

Solution. In Problem 5.6 we proved the special case for the Poisson process. For fixed t, define

$$P_n(i) = \text{pr}\{Z_\tau = i \quad \text{at times } \tau = t/n, 2t/n, \ldots, (n-1)t/n, t \mid Z_0 = i\}$$
$$= \{p_{ii}(t/n)\}^n \quad \text{by the Markov property and time independence}$$
$$= \{1 - q_i t/n + O(t^2/n^2)\}^n \to e^{-q_i t} \quad \text{as } n \to \infty$$

But, as $n \to \infty$, $P_n(i) \to \text{pr}\{Z_\tau = i \quad (0 \leqslant \tau \leqslant t)\} = \text{pr}(T_i > t)$. Therefore
$$\text{pr}(T_i \leqslant t) = 1 - e^{-q_i t}, \text{ the df of an } \mathcal{E}(q_i) \text{ rv.} \qquad \square$$

If $0 \leqslant q_i < \infty$, then state i is called *stable*; if $q_i = \infty$, then i is called *instantaneous*; and if $q_i = 0$, then i is *absorbing*. By Problem 6.1 a particle instantaneously jumps from an instantaneous state, and never leaves an absorbing one.

The *Kolmogorov differential equations* relate $\mathbf{P}(t)$ to $\mathbf{Q}$. The *backward* equations are
$$\frac{d\mathbf{P}(t)}{dt} = \mathbf{Q}\mathbf{P}(t)$$
i.e.
$$p'_{ij}(t) = \sum_{k \in S} q_{ik} p_{kj}(t)$$

and are generally valid. The *forward* equations are
$$\frac{d\mathbf{P}(t)}{dt} = \mathbf{P}(t)\mathbf{Q}$$
i.e.
$$p'_{ij}(t) = \sum_{k \in S} p_{ik}(t) q_{kj}$$

and these do not always hold.

6.2 Applications

Problem 6.2 *The general time-independent birth and death process with immigration.* Consider the Markov chain $\{Z_t : t \in [0, \infty)\}$, where Z_t is the population size at a time t. If $Z_t = i$ $(i = 0, 1, 2, \ldots)$, then in a short time interval $(t, t+\Delta)$, Z_t increases by one (by a birth or the arrival of an immigrant) with probability $\lambda_i \Delta + o(\Delta)$, decreases by one (by a death or the departure of an emigrant) with probability $\mu_i \Delta + o(\Delta)$, or does not change with probability $1 - (\lambda_i + \mu_i)\Delta + o(\Delta)$. Any other changes must therefore have probability $o(\Delta)$. Clearly $\mu_0 = 0$. What is the matrix $\mathbf{Q}$?

Find the Kolmogorov forward differential equations, and determine their equilibrium solution if it exists.

Solution. The state space is $\{0, 1, 2, \ldots\}$. Since the transition matrix $\mathbf{P}(\Delta)$ is

$$\text{pr}(Z_{t+\Delta} = j \mid Z_t = i) = \begin{cases} \lambda_i \Delta + o(\Delta) & (j = i+1) \\ 1 - (\lambda_i + \mu_i)\Delta + o(\Delta) & (j = i) \\ \mu_i \Delta + o(\Delta) & (j = i-1) \\ o(\Delta) & (\text{otherwise}) \end{cases} \qquad (6.4)$$

we have that

$$
\mathbf{Q} = \begin{array}{c} \\ 0 \\ 1 \\ 2 \\ 3 \\ \vdots \end{array}
\begin{pmatrix}
\overset{0}{-\lambda_0} & \overset{1}{\lambda_0} & \overset{2}{0} & \overset{3}{0} & \overset{4}{0} & \cdots \\
\mu_1 & -\mu_1-\lambda_1 & \lambda_1 & 0 & 0 & \cdots \\
0 & \mu_2 & -\mu_2-\lambda_2 & \lambda_2 & 0 & \cdots \\
0 & 0 & \mu_3 & -\mu_3-\lambda_3 & \lambda_3 & \cdots \\
\vdots & \vdots & \vdots & \vdots & \vdots &
\end{pmatrix}
$$

Let us abbreviate $p_{ij}(t)$ to p_{ij}, and use p'_{ij} to denote $(d/dt)p_{ij}(t)$. Then, if $Z_t = i$, the forward equations are

$$p'_{i0} = -\lambda_0 p_{i0} + \mu_1 p_{i1}$$
$$p'_{ij} = \lambda_{j-1}p_{i,j-1} - (\mu_j+\lambda_j)p_{ij} + \mu_{j+1}p_{i,j+1} \quad (j = 1,2,\ldots) \tag{6.5}$$

For the equilibrium solution, let $p_{ij}(t) \to \pi_j$ as $t \to \infty$, then

$$0 = -\lambda_0\pi_0 + \mu_1\pi_1$$
$$0 = (\lambda_{j-1}\pi_{j-1}-\mu_j\pi_j)-(\lambda_j\pi_j-\mu_{j+1}\pi_{j+1}) \quad (j = 1,2,\ldots)$$

Write
$$I_j = \lambda_j\pi_j - \mu_{j+1}\pi_{j+1} \quad (j = 0,1,2,\ldots)$$

Then
$$0 = -I_0$$
$$0 = I_{j-1}-I_j \quad (j = 1,2,\ldots)$$

so
$$I_j = 0 \quad (j = 0,1,2,\ldots)$$

Therefore
$$\pi_{j+1}/\pi_j = \lambda_j/\mu_{j+1}$$

Therefore
$$\pi_j = (\pi_j/\pi_{j-1})(\pi_{j-1}/\pi_{j-2})\ldots(\pi_1/\pi_0)\pi_0 = v_j\pi_0$$

where
$$v_j = \frac{\lambda_{j-1}\lambda_{j-2}\ldots\lambda_0}{\mu_j\mu_{j-1}\ldots\mu_1}, \qquad v_0 = 1 \tag{6.6}$$

Then, since $\Sigma\pi_j = 1$,

$$1 = \pi_0 \sum_{j=0}^{\infty} v_j,$$

so
$$\pi_j = v_j / \sum_{k=0}^{\infty} v_k \quad (j = 0,1,2,\ldots) \tag{6.7}$$

This will be a probability distribution if and only if Σv_k converges. ☐

Problem 6.3 *The linear birth and death process with immigration.* Consider a population process $\{Z_t : t \in [0,\infty)\}$, where Z_t is the size of the population at time t. People in the population behave independently of one another. In any short time interval of length Δ, with probability $\lambda\Delta + o(\Delta)$ a member will give birth to another member, with probability $\mu\Delta + o(\Delta)$ the member will die or emigrate, and with probability $1 - (\lambda + \mu)\Delta + o(\Delta)$ nothing will happen to the member. In Δ also, an immigrant will join the population with probability $\alpha\Delta + o(\Delta)$. If initially the population contains i members, what is the pgf, $\Pi_t(s)$, for Z_t?

Solution. We consider a decomposition based on the last Δ. Then

$$Z_{t+\Delta} = Z_t + X_1 + \ldots + X_{Z_t} + W$$

where

$$W = \begin{cases} 1 & \text{if there is an immigrant in } (t, t+\Delta), \text{ i.e. with probability } \alpha\Delta + o(\Delta) \\ 0 & \text{otherwise, i.e. with probability } 1 - \alpha\Delta + o(\Delta) \end{cases}$$

and

$$X_l = \begin{cases} 1 & \text{if the } l\text{th member gives birth in } (t, t+\Delta), \text{ i.e. with probability } \\ & \lambda\Delta + o(\Delta) \\ -1 & \text{if the } l\text{th member dies or emigrates in } (t, t+\Delta), \text{ i.e. with} \\ & \text{probability } \mu\Delta + o(\Delta) \\ 0 & \text{otherwise, i.e. with probability } 1 - (\lambda + \mu)\Delta + o(\Delta). \end{cases}$$

Then
$$Es^W = \alpha\Delta s^1 + (1 - \alpha\Delta)s^0 + o(\Delta) = 1 - (\alpha - \alpha s)\Delta + o(\Delta)$$

and
$$Es^{X_l} = \lambda\Delta s^1 + \{1 - (\lambda + \mu)\Delta\}s^0 + \mu\Delta s^{-1} + o(\Delta)$$
$$= 1 + \{\lambda s - (\lambda + \mu) + \mu s^{-1}\}\Delta + o(\Delta)$$

Therefore
$$Es^{X_1 + \ldots + X_i + W} = (Es^{X_1})(Es^{X_2})\ldots(Es^{X_i})(Es^W) = (Es^{X_l})^i(Es^W)$$
$$= \{(i\lambda + \alpha)\Delta + o(\Delta)\}s + \{1 - (i\lambda + i\mu + \alpha)\Delta + o(\Delta)\} + \{i\mu\Delta + o(\Delta)\}s^{-1} + o(\Delta)$$
from the expansion and collection of terms which are $O(1)$ and $O(\Delta)$.
Therefore
$$\text{pr}(Z_{t+\Delta} = j \mid Z_t = i) = \text{pr}(X_1 + \ldots + X_i + W = j - i)$$
$$= \begin{cases} (i\lambda + \alpha)\Delta + o(\Delta) & (j = i+1) \\ 1 - (i\lambda + i\mu + \alpha)\Delta + o(\Delta) & (j = i) \\ i\mu\Delta + o(\Delta) & (j = i-1) \\ o(\Delta) & (\text{otherwise}) \end{cases}$$

It is clear that we could have written this, or equivalently the **Q**-matrix, straight down. It is of the form (6.4), with $\lambda_i = i\lambda + \alpha$, $\mu_i = i\mu$, and so equations 6.5 are

$$p'_{i0} = -\alpha p_{i0} + \mu p_{i1}$$
$$p'_{ij} = \{(j-1)\lambda + \alpha\}p_{i,j-1} - \{j(\lambda + \mu) + \alpha\}p_{ij} + (j+1)\mu p_{i,j+1} \quad (j = 1, 2, \ldots)$$
$$(6.8)$$

A useful device is to set $p_{ij} \equiv 0$ for $j = \ldots, -2, -1$ (clearly true), then equations 6.8 hold for $j = \ldots, -1, 0, 1, 2, \ldots$. We multiply equations 6.8 by s^j:

$$p'_{ij}s^j = \lambda s^2 (j-1)s^{j-2}p_{i,j-1} + \alpha s s^{j-1}p_{i,j-1} - (\lambda+\mu)sjs^{j-1}p_{ij} - \alpha s^j p_{ij}$$
$$+ \mu(j+1)s^j p_{i,j+1}$$

We then sum over $j = \ldots, -1, 0, 1, 2, \ldots$, and abbreviate to Π the pgf

$$\Pi_t(s) = \mathrm{E}_{Z_t|Z_0 = i}s^{Z_t} = \sum_{j=-\infty}^{\infty} p_{ij}(t)s^j$$

Then

$$\frac{\partial \Pi}{\partial t} = \lambda s^2 \frac{\partial \Pi}{\partial s} + \alpha s \Pi - (\lambda+\mu)s\frac{\partial \Pi}{\partial s} - \alpha \Pi + \mu \frac{\partial \Pi}{\partial s}$$

i.e.

$$\frac{\partial \Pi}{\partial t} + (\lambda s - \mu)(1-s)\frac{\partial \Pi}{\partial s} = \alpha(s-1)\Pi \qquad (6.9)$$

We shall solve this partial differential equation for Π. We shall not discuss here why the method works. We solve the *auxiliary equations*

$$\frac{dt}{1} = \frac{ds}{(\lambda s - \mu)(1-s)} = \frac{d\Pi}{-\alpha(1-s)\Pi}$$

We shall suppose $\lambda \neq \mu$ (Exercise 5 is the case $\lambda = \mu$), then

$$(\lambda - \mu)dt = \frac{\lambda ds}{\lambda s - \mu} + \frac{ds}{1-s} = d\log\left|\frac{\lambda s - \mu}{1-s}\right|$$

$$\frac{\lambda s - \mu}{1-s}e^{-(\lambda - \mu)t} = \text{constant}$$

and

$$\left(\frac{\alpha}{\lambda}\right)\left(\frac{\lambda ds}{\lambda s - \mu}\right) = -\frac{d\Pi}{\Pi}$$

Therefore

$$(\lambda s - \mu)^{\alpha/\lambda}\Pi = \text{constant}$$

Since the partial differential equation is of the first order, it can have only one arbitrary constant, so the two constants must be functions of one another, i.e.

$$(\lambda s - \mu)^{\alpha/\lambda}\Pi = f\left\{\frac{\lambda s - \mu}{1-s}e^{-(\lambda - \mu)t}\right\} \qquad (6.10)$$

We determine f from the initial condition: $Z_0 = i$, i.e. $\Pi_0(s) = s^i$.

$$(\lambda s - \mu)^{\alpha/\lambda}s^i = f\left(\frac{\lambda s - \mu}{1-s}\right)$$

By setting $r = (\lambda s - \mu)/(1-s)$, so $s = (\mu + r)/(\lambda + r)$, we determine the function $f(r)$. This, when substituted into (6.10) gives $\Pi = \Pi_t(s)$. $\qquad \square$

Alternatively, given $Z_0 = i$, Z_t has the same distribution as $Z_t^* + Y_t^{(1)} + \ldots + Y_t^{(i)}$, where Z_t^* is the number of immigrants who arrived in $(0, t)$ and are still present at time t plus their descendants who are still present at time t, and

$$Y_t^{(j)} = \begin{cases} 1 & \text{if the } j\text{th of the } i \text{ original members is still present at time } t \\ 0 & \text{otherwise} \end{cases} \qquad (j = 1, 2, \ldots, i)$$

Then Z_t^* and each of the $Y_t^{(j)}$ are mutually independent, and Z_t^* is distributed like Z_t given $Z_0 = 0$. Also, each $Y_t^{(j)}$ is a Bernoulli rv with probability of success, $\mathrm{pr}(T > t) = \mathrm{e}^{-\mu t}$ (by Problem 5.5) Therefore

$$\Pi_t(s) = \mathrm{E}s^{Z_t^* + Y_t^{(1)} + \ldots + Y_t^{(i)}} = \mathrm{E}_{Z_t|Z_0=0}\, s^{Z_t}(1 - \mathrm{e}^{-\mu t} + \mathrm{e}^{-\mu t}s)^i$$

We need therefore have considered only the case $i = 0$.

Special cases have been given names:

$\lambda = \mu = 0$: the *Poisson process*

$\lambda = 0$: the *immigration-emigration process*

$\alpha = \mu = 0$: the *linear growth process* or the *Yule process*

$\alpha = 0$: the *linear birth and death process*

Problem 6.4   Find $\mathrm{E}Z_t$ for the population process of Problem 6.3.

Solution. We can find $\mathrm{E}Z_t$ and $\mathrm{V}Z_t$ from the pgf $\Pi_t(s)$. However, it is not necessary to solve equation 6.9 to determine them. If we differentiate equation 6.9 with respect to s, we obtain

$$\frac{\partial^2 \Pi}{\partial s \partial t} + (\lambda s - \mu)(1 - s)\frac{\partial^2 \Pi}{\partial s^2} + \{(\lambda s - \mu)(-1) + \lambda(1 - s) - \alpha(s - 1)\}\frac{\partial \Pi}{\partial s} = \alpha \Pi$$

$$(6.11)$$

Now
$$\Pi_t(1) = 1, \qquad \left.\frac{\partial \Pi}{\partial s}\right|_{s=1} = M_t = \mathrm{E}Z_t$$

and
$$\left.\frac{\partial^2 \Pi}{\partial s \partial t}\right|_{s=1} = \left.\frac{\partial}{\partial t}\left(\frac{\partial \Pi}{\partial s}\right)\right|_{s=1} = \frac{dM_t}{dt}$$

if we assume that

$$\lim_{s \to 1}\frac{\partial}{\partial t} = \frac{\partial}{\partial t}\lim_{s \to 1}$$

Letting $s \to 1$ in equation 6.11 we thus obtain a first-order ordinary differential equation in M_t:

$$\frac{dM_t}{dt} + (\mu - \lambda)M_t = \alpha \qquad (6.12)$$

Then, since $M_0 = \mathrm{E}Z_0 = i$,

$$M_t = \frac{\alpha}{\mu - \lambda} + \left(i - \frac{\alpha}{\mu - \lambda}\right)e^{-(\mu - \lambda)t} \qquad \qquad \square \quad (6.13)$$

Since

$$\left.\frac{\partial^3 \Pi}{\partial^2 s \partial t}\right|_{s=1} = \frac{\partial}{\partial t}\left(\frac{\partial^2 \Pi}{\partial s^2}\right)\bigg|_{s=1} = \frac{d}{dt}\,\mathrm{E}\{Z_t(Z_t - 1)\} = \frac{d}{dt}(V_t + M_t^2 - M_t)$$

$$= \frac{dV_t}{dt} + (2M_t - 1)\frac{dM_t}{dt}$$

where $V_t = \mathrm{V}Z_t$, we can differentiate a tidied-up equation 6.11 with respect to s, and let $s \to 1$, to obtain a first-order ordinary differential equation for V_t, into which we can substitute for M_t from equation 6.13. Note that $V_0 = \mathrm{V}Z_0 = 0$.

Problem 6.5 *The single-server queue with Poisson arrivals and exponential service times.* Customers arrive in a Poisson process of rate λ, and join the queue. The service times for customers are independent $\mathscr{E}(\mu)$ rvs. Determine a partial differential equation for $\Pi_t(s)$, the pgf for Z_t, the number of customers in the queue (including the one being served, if any) at time t. Find the equilibrium distribution of the queue size.

Solution. In $(t, t + \Delta)$,

$$\mathrm{pr}(\text{a new customer arrives}) = \lambda\Delta + o(\Delta)$$
$$\mathrm{pr}(\text{a customer finishes being served and he leaves}) = \mu\Delta + o(\Delta)$$
$$\mathrm{pr}(\text{no customer arrives and none completes being served})$$
$$= 1 - (\lambda + \mu)\Delta + o(\Delta)$$
$$\mathrm{pr}(\text{anything else}) = o(\Delta)$$

Let $p_k(t) = \mathrm{pr}(Z_t = k)$, and abbreviate it to p_k. The forward equations are

$$p_0' = -\lambda p_0 + \mu p_1$$
$$p_k' = \lambda p_{k-1} - (\mu + \lambda)p_k + \mu p_{k+1} \quad (k = 1, 2, \dots)$$

Multiply the kth equation by s^k and sum over $k = 0, 1, 2, \dots$; abbreviate $\Pi_t(s)$ to Π; then

$$\frac{\partial \Pi}{\partial t} = \lambda s\Pi - \mu(\Pi - p_0) - \lambda\Pi + \frac{\mu}{s}(\Pi - p_0) = \left(\frac{s-1}{s}\right)\{(\lambda s - \mu)\Pi + \mu p_0\}$$

If $p_k(t) \to \pi_k$ as $t \to \infty$, then $\Pi \to \sum_{k=0}^{\infty} \pi_k s^k$, and $\{\pi_k\}$ is given by setting $\frac{\partial \Pi}{\partial t} = 0$. Therefore

$$\sum_{k=0}^{\infty} \pi_k s^k = \frac{\mu\pi_0}{\mu - \lambda s} = \pi_0 \sum_{k=0}^{\infty} \left(\frac{\lambda}{\mu}\right)^k s^k$$

Therefore

$$\pi_k = (1-\rho)\rho^k \quad (k = 0, 1, 2, \ldots)$$

where

$$\rho = \frac{\lambda}{\mu} = \frac{\mu^{-1}}{\lambda^{-1}} = \text{E(service time)/E(arrival interval)}$$

is the traffic intensity. Then π_k is a probability only if $\rho < 1$. For $\rho < 1$ the sequence $\{\pi_k\}$ is the geometric distribution $\mathcal{G}(\rho)$. ☐

Alternatively, equation 6.7 gives this result with $\lambda_j = \lambda$, $\mu_j = \mu$.

This queue is in fact a random walk in continuous time with steps $+1$, -1, having probabilities $\lambda/(\lambda+\mu)$, $\mu/(\lambda+\mu)$ respectively, and steps taking place as a Poisson process of rate $\lambda+\mu$. There is an impenetrable barrier at the origin at which the particle stays for a time which is an $\mathscr{E}(\lambda)$ rv and then jumps to $+1$.

EXERCISES

1 *Accident proneness.* Suppose that if no previous accidents have occurred the probability of an accident in $(t, t+\varDelta)$ is $\alpha\varDelta + o(\varDelta)$, but that it is $\beta\varDelta + o(\varDelta)$ otherwise, regardless of how many earlier accidents there have been. If $\beta < \alpha$, then the model represents the case in which the lesson has been learnt, but if $\beta > \alpha$ then we have the case in which the shock leads to a state in which more blunders are likely. Find the Kolmogorov forward differential equations for $p_k(t) = \text{pr}(N_t = k)$, where N_t is the number of accidents in $(0, t)$, and show that $\varPi_t(s)$, the pgf for N_t, satisfies

$$\frac{\partial\varPi}{\partial t} + \beta(1-s)\varPi = (\beta-\alpha)(1-s)\,e^{-\alpha t}$$

Find $\text{E}N_t$ from this equation (by the method of Problem 6.4). Note that this model reduces to the Poisson process when $\alpha = \beta$.

2. Suppose that the probability of an accident in $(t, t+\varDelta)$ given that k accidents have already occurred is $(\alpha+k\lambda)\varDelta + o(\varDelta)$ $(k = 0, 1, 2, \ldots)$. Find the Kolmogorov forward differential equations for $p_j(t)$ in this case. Verify that they are the same as for a linear birth process with immigration, the birth rate per individual being λ and the immigration rate being α. Solve the equations to show that N_t has a negative binomial distribution.

3. *Race relations.* For the linear birth process with immigration of Exercise 2, show that if there are n individuals present at time zero, then the population size at time t has pgf

$$s^n\{e^{\lambda t}-s(e^{\lambda t}-1)\}^{-n-\alpha/\lambda}$$

If the individuals present at time zero and their descendants are called *natives*, and those who enter after time zero and their descendants are called *immigrants*, prove that if $n\lambda > \alpha$ the expected number of natives always exceeds the expected number of immigrants.

4. *The linear birth and death process.* If there is no immigration and if the birth rate per individual is λ and the death rate per individual is μ ($\lambda \neq \mu$), show that the population size at time t, Z_t, has pgf $(a-b\psi)/(a-c\psi)$, if initially $Z_0 = 1$, where $a = \lambda s - \mu$, $b = (s-1)\mu$, $c = (s-1)\lambda$, $\psi = \exp\{(\lambda-\mu)t\}$. Determine EZ_t, VZ_t and the probability of extinction.

5. Do Exercise 4 and Problem 6.3 for the cases in which $\lambda = \mu$. Check that the results could have been derived by setting $\mu = \lambda + \varepsilon$ in the solutions for $\lambda \neq \mu$, and letting $\varepsilon \to 0$.

6. Find VZ_t for the population process of Problem 6.3, using the method outlined following the solution to Problem 6.4.

7. Consider a community in which there is competition for food. If the community contains i ($i = 0, 1, 2, \ldots, n$) members at time t, then, during a short interval $(t, t+\Delta)$, a new member joins with probability $(n-i)\lambda\Delta + o(\Delta)$; each member independently leaves with probability $\lambda\Delta + o(\Delta)$, and there is no change in membership with probability $1 - n\lambda\Delta + o(\Delta)$. Set out the Kolmogorov forward differential equations for the distribution of the size, Z_t, of the community at time t.

If initially the community had no members, show that Z_t is Bin $(n, \frac{1}{2}(1-e^{-2\lambda t}))$.

8. The incoming traffic to a car park with n spaces is a Poisson process of rate λ, but only while spaces remain unfilled. In any short time interval of length Δ each vehicle already in the car park independently leaves with probability $v\Delta + o(\Delta)$. Write down the Kolmogorov forward differential equations for the distribution of the number, Z_t, of spaces filled at time t.

Find the equilibrium distribution of Z_t. If the car park is large enough that there is always room for incoming traffic, and if initially k spaces are filled, find EZ_t.

9. *A single-server queue with constant service times.* Customers arrive in a Poisson process of rate λ, and the service time is unity. Let rv Z_t be the number of waiting customers, including the one being served, at time t. Show that if Y_t customers arrive in time interval $(t, t+1)$ then

$$Z_{t+1} = \begin{cases} Z_t - 1 + Y_t & (Z_t = 1, 2, \ldots) \\ Y_t & (Z_t = 0) \end{cases}$$

Find recurrence relations for $p_k(t) = \mathrm{pr}(Z_t = k)$, and show that if $G_t(s)$ is the pgf for Z_t, then

$$s\, G_{t+1}(s) = \{(s-1)p_0(t) + G_t(s)\}\, \exp\{\lambda(s-1)\}$$

(See Problem 4.12 and Exercises 3 and 4 of Chapter 4.)

Chapter 7

Non-Markov Processes in Continuous Time with Discrete State Spaces

We now consider population processes for which the lifetimes of members are not necessarily exponential rvs. The remaining lifetime of an individual will depend on how old he is now, and so the future size of the population will depend not only on its present size, but also on the present ages of its members. The process is still Markovian if we include this information, but we would not wish to keep records on every individual throughout their lives. There is no change in the population size except when an event occurs: when a child is born, or someone dies, or an immigrant arrives or an emigrant departs. We consider, therefore, decompositions based on the times of the first or last of these events.

7.1 Renewal theory We consider first the special case of a *renewal process*. The function of a single component—for example, a continuously burning light bulb—is observed and it is replaced by another immediately it fails. The components will have lifetimes which are independent rvs $\{X_i\}$, each distributed like a positive rv X. Then the rv Z_n, the time to the failure of the nth component if the first is fitted at time 0, is given by the random walk

$$Z_n = X_1 + \ldots + X_n, \qquad Z_0 = 0$$

See Figure 7.1. We take a fixed time t and are interested in the following rvs:

the number of renewals in $(0, t]$, $N_t = \max\{n : Z_n \leqslant t\}$
the forward recurrence time, $T_t^+ = Z_{N_t+1} - t$
and the backward recurrence time, $T_t^- = t - Z_{N_t}$

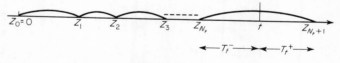

Figure 7.1

Now, for a fixed t,

$$T_t^- + T_t^+ = Z_{N_t+1} - Z_{N_t} = X_{N_t+1}$$

is not distributed as X, since in any realisation of the process the fixed

77

t is more likely to be in a long interval than in a short one. This makes the process non-Markov since T_t^+ depends on T_t^-. For example, if a light bulb can be of two qualities—a defective one which lasts generally less than a week or a good one which lasts about a year—then, if a bulb has already survived 6 months, it is of proven quality with about another 6 months' lifetime.

There is an important and fundamental relationship between the counting process $\{N_t : t \in (0, \infty)\}$ and the random walk process $\{Z_n : n = 0, 1, 2, \ldots\}$. The events 'the number of renewals in time t is at least n' and 'the time to the nth renewal does not exceed t' are the same, and so have the same probability. Therefore

$$\operatorname{pr}(N_t \geqslant n) = \operatorname{pr}(Z_n \leqslant t) \tag{7.1}$$

Suppose that $EX = \mu$, $VX = \sigma^2$. We can approximate the distribution of N_t for large t by working directly with Z_n; that is,

$$\operatorname{pr}(N_t < n) = 1 - \operatorname{pr}(Z_n \leqslant t) = 1 - \operatorname{pr}(Y \leqslant (t - n\mu)/\sigma\sqrt{n})$$

where, by the central limit theorem, rv Y is approximately $N(0, 1)$. By the law of large numbers $n^{-1}Z_n \to \mu$ as $n \to \infty$, and from this we can show that $N_t \sim t/\mu$ as $t \to \infty$.

Suppose that X is a continuous rv with density $f(x)$ $(0 < x < \infty)$.

***Problem* 7.1**   Determine an integral equation for the pgf, $\Pi_t(s)$, for N_t.

Solution. We use a decomposition based on the time U of the first renewal. If $U > t$, then $N_t = 0$; if $U = u < t$, then $N_t = 1 + N'_{t-u}$, where N'_{t-u} is the number of further renewals in the remaining $t - u$ up to t, and so is distributed like N_{t-u}. We are using the fact that *the Markov property holds at renewal points*, since then it is as though the process were starting off again. Now $\operatorname{pr}\{U \in (u, u + du)\} = f(u)du$. Therefore

$$Es^{N_t} = E_U E_{N_t|U=u} s^{N_t} = \int_0^\infty f(u)\, du\, E_{N_t|U=u} s^{N_t}$$

$$= \int_0^t f(u)\, du\, Es^{1+N_{t-u}} + \int_t^\infty f(u)du\, Es^0$$

i.e. $$\Pi_t(s) = s \int_0^t f(u)\Pi_{t-u}(s)\, du + \int_t^\infty f(u)\, du \tag{7.2} \qquad \square$$

***Problem* 7.2**   Determine integral equations for the *renewal function* $H_t = EN_t$, and the *renewal density* $h_t = (d/dt)\, H_t$.

Solution. We differentiate equation 7.2 with respect to s, and let $s \to 1$.

Then

$$\frac{\partial \Pi_t(s)}{\partial s} = \int_0^t f(u)\Pi_{t-u}(s)\, du + s\int_0^t f(u)\frac{\partial \Pi_{t-u}(s)}{\partial t}\, du$$

Therefore

$$H_t = \int_0^t f(u)\, du + \int_0^t f(u)H_{t-u}\, du$$

We differentiate this with respect to t:

$$h_t = f(t) + f(t)H_0 + \int_0^t f(u)h_{t-u}\, du$$

$$= f(t) + \int_0^t f(u)h_{t-u}\, du \tag{7.3}$$

since $H_0 = EN_0 = E0 = 0$. $\qquad\square$

Since $N_t \sim t/\mu$ as $t \to \infty$, $H_t \sim t/\mu$ and $h_t \sim 1/\mu$.

Problem 7.3 Show that h_t is the *instantaneous transition rate* defined by

$$\mathrm{pr}\{\text{a renewal occurs in } (t, t+\varDelta)\,|\,\text{a renewal occurred at } 0\}$$
$$= h_t\varDelta + o(\varDelta)$$

Solution. If we write equation 7.3 in the form

$$h_t\varDelta + o(\varDelta) = \{f(t)\varDelta + o(\varDelta)\} + \int_0^t \{f(u)\, du\}\{h_{t-u}\varDelta + o(\varDelta)\}$$

then the right side is

pr{the first renewal is in $(t, t+\varDelta)$ or it is in $(u, u+du)$ for some $u \in (0, t)$ and there is a renewal in an interval of length $\varDelta$ after a further $t-u$}

i.e. it is the probability that there is a renewal in $(t, t+\varDelta)$ given there was a renewal at 0. $\qquad\square$

Problem 7.4 When the lifetime rv is $\mathscr{E}(\lambda)$, that is, exponential with parameter λ, show that rv N_t is $\mathscr{P}(\lambda t)$, that is, Poisson with mean λt, and that h_t is λ.

Solution. We use the definition of h_t given by Problem 7.3. If h_t is λ, then by Problem 5.2 N_t is $\mathscr{P}(\lambda t)$, and by Problem 5.6 the intervals between events are $\mathscr{E}(\lambda)$.

The other way round: we put

$$f(u) = \lambda e^{-\lambda u} \quad (0 < u < \infty)$$

into equation 7.2. Then

$$\Pi_t(s) = s\int_0^t \lambda e^{-\lambda u}\Pi_{t-u}(s)\, du + \int_t^\infty \lambda e^{-\lambda u}\, du$$

G

79

We multiply by $e^{\lambda t}$, set $v = t-u$ in the first integral, and write
$$A_t = e^{\lambda t}\Pi_t(s)$$
keeping s fixed. Then
$$A_t = \lambda s \int_0^t A_v \, dv + 1$$
We now differentiate with respect to t
$$\frac{dA_t}{dt} = \lambda s A_t$$

Therefore
$$A_t = e^{\lambda st}, \quad \text{since } A_0 = \Pi_0(s) = E s^{N_0} = 1$$
Therefore
$$\Pi_t(s) = e^{-\lambda t}A_t = e^{-\lambda t(1-s)}$$
the pgf of the $\mathscr{P}(\lambda t)$ distribution. Then $H_t = EN_t = \lambda t$, so $h_t = H'_t = \lambda$. $\square$

Problem 7.5 Find the distribution of the forward recurrence time T_t^+ of a renewal process, and the limit of this distribution as $t \to \infty$.

Solution. We use the method of Problem 7.3 to find the density $g_t^+(x)$ of T_t^+ by a decomposition based on the last renewal before t.

$\text{pr}\{T_t^+ \in (x, x+\Delta)\}$

  = pr{the first renewal is in $(t+x, t+x+\Delta)(x > 0)$, or the last
      renewal before t is in $(v, v+dv)(0 < v < t)$ for some $v \in (0, t)$, and
      the next renewal is in $(t+x, t+x+\Delta)$ i.e. in $(t+x-v, t+x-v+\Delta)$
                                                                          later}

i.e. $g_t^+(x)\Delta + o(\Delta) = \{f(t+x)\Delta + o(\Delta)\} + \int_0^t h_v \, dv \, \{f(t+x-v)\Delta + o(\Delta)\}.$

We set $u = t-v$ in the integral, divide by Δ, and let $\Delta \to 0$. Then
$$g_t^+(x) = f(t+x) + \int_0^t h_{t-u}f(u+x) \, du \tag{7.4}$$

We must suppose that $f(x) \to 0$ as $x \to \infty$. Equation 7.4 is true for fixed t. Let $t \to \infty$, then $h_{t-u} \to \mu^{-1}$, so
$$g_t^+(x) \to g(x) = \int_0^\infty \frac{1}{\mu}f(u+x) \, du = \frac{1}{\mu}\int_x^\infty f(w) \, dw = \frac{1}{\mu}\{1-F(x)\} \quad \square$$

Problem 7.6 Find the distribution of the backward recurrence time T_t^-, and its limit as $t \to \infty$.

Solution.

$\text{pr}\{T_t^- \in (x, x+\Delta)\}$

$$= \text{pr}\{\text{there is no renewal in } (0, t), \text{ in which case } T_t^- = t, \text{ or there is a}$$
renewal in $(t-x, t-x+\varDelta)\,(0 < x < t)$ and there are no more
$$\text{renewals in } (t-x, t)\}$$

Now $\text{pr}\{\text{no renewal in } (u, v)\,|\,\text{a renewal at } u\} = \text{pr}(X > v-u) = 1-F(v-u)$.
Therefore
$$\text{pr}(T_t^- = t) = \text{pr}(X > t) = 1-F(t)$$
$$g_t^-(x) = h_{t-x}\{1-F(x)\} \quad (0 < x < t)$$

That is, the distribution of T_t^- is an atom of probability of amount $1-F(t)$ at t and a density $g_t^-(x)$ over $(0, t)$. As $t \to \infty, F(t) \to 1$ and $h_{t-x} \to \mu^{-1}$, therefore the distribution of T_t^- tends to a density $g(x) = \{1-F(x)\}/\mu$ $(0 < x < \infty)$, the same limiting distribution as that of T_t^+. $\qquad\square$

7.2 Population processes If instead of replacing a failed component by another we replace it with X components, where X is an rv having pgf $G(s)$, then the situation is that of the family tree described in Problem 4.14, except that the lifetimes of individuals are independent rvs each having density $f(x)\,(0 < x < \infty)$.

***Problem* 7.7** *The continuous-time branching process.* Suppose that at time 0 the process starts with the birth of a single individual, the founder. Find an integral equation for the pgf, $\Pi_t(s)$, of the size, Z_t, at time t, of the population.

Solution. We consider a decomposition based on the time, U, of the founder's death. Let N be the number of offspring left by the founder. Then $E_N s^N = G(s)$. If $U = u$, then, for $t < u$, $Z_t = Z_0 = 1$; but for $t > u$
$$Z_t = \begin{cases} Z_{t-u}^{(1)} + \ldots + Z_{t-u}^{(N)} & (N = 1, 2, \ldots) \\ 0 & (N = 0) \end{cases}$$
where each $Z_{t-u}^{(j)}$ is independently distributed like Z_{t-u}. Therefore, for $t > u$, by Problem 2.14,
$$E_{Z_t|U=u<t} s^{Z_t} = G\{\Pi_{t-u}(s)\}$$
Therefore
$$\Pi_t(s) = E_{Z_t} s^{Z_t} = E_U E_{Z_t|U=U} s^{Z_t} = \int_0^\infty f(u)\,du\, E_{Z_t|U=u} s^{Z_t}$$
$$= \int_0^t f(u)\,du\, G\{\Pi_{t-u}(s)\}\,du + \int_t^\infty f(u)\,du\, Es^1$$
$$= s\{1-F(t)\} + \int_0^t f(u)G\{\Pi_{t-u}(s)\}\,du \qquad\square \quad (7.5)$$

***Problem* 7.8** Determine $\Pi_t(s)$ in the special case in which the number of offspring is always 2 and the lifetime rv is $\mathscr{E}(\lambda)$.

Solution. After an exponential interval each branch splits into two new branches, so $G(s) = s^2$ and $f(u) = \lambda e^{-\lambda u}$ $(0 < u < \infty)$. This is the *linear growth process*, a special case of Problem 6.3. Equation 7.5 becomes

$$\Pi_t(s) = se^{-\lambda t} + \int_0^t \lambda e^{-\lambda u}\{\Pi_{t-u}(s)\}^2\, du$$

Multiply by $e^{\lambda t}$, set $v = t - u$ in the integral, differentiate with respect to t, divide out $e^{\lambda t}$, and abbreviate $\Pi_t(s)$ to Π. Then

$$\frac{d\Pi}{dt} = \lambda\Pi(\Pi - 1),$$

i.e.
$$\lambda\, dt = \frac{d\Pi}{\Pi(\Pi - 1)} = \left(\frac{1}{\Pi - 1} - \frac{1}{\Pi}\right) d\Pi = d\log\frac{|\Pi - 1|}{\Pi}$$

so
$$\log\frac{|\Pi - 1|}{\Pi} = \lambda t + \text{constant}$$

Now $\Pi_0(s) = s$, so $\Pi_t(s) = \dfrac{se^{-\lambda t}}{1 - (1 - e^{-\lambda t})s}$,

i.e. $Z_t - 1$ is $\mathscr{G}(e^{-\lambda t})$, a geometrically distributed rv. ☐

7.3 Queuing theory
Problem 7.9 *Waiting-time distributions.* Suppose that the time intervals between the arrivals of customers are independently and identically distributed continuous rvs, that the service times of customers are independently and identically distributed rvs, and that there is just a single server. Label the kth customer C_k. Denote by Y_k the time between the arrivals of C_k and C_{k+1}; by X_k the service time of C_k; and by W_k the waiting time (which excludes the time in which he is being served) of C_k. If the density of the rv $V_k = X_k - Y_k$ is $g(v)$ $(-\infty < v < \infty)$, and the distribution function of W_k is $F_k(w)$, show that

$$F_{k+1}(w) = \int_{-\infty}^{w} F_k(w - v)g(v)\, dv$$

Solution. Assume that C_1 arrives at $t = 0$ and finds no one ahead of him; therefore $W_1 = 0$. Customer C_k is in the queue for a time $W_k + X_k$. If $Y_k > W_k + X_k$, then $W_{k+1} = 0$; that is, if C_{k+1} arrives late enough he has no waiting. If $Y_k \leqslant W_k + X_k$, then $W_{k+1} = W_k + X_k - Y_k = W_k + V_k$. That is, $W_{k+1} = \max(W_k + V_k, 0)$. Now $F_k(w) = 0$ $(w < 0,$ for all $k)$. Therefore, for $w \geqslant 0$,

$$F_{k+1}(w) = \mathrm{pr}(W_{k+1} \leqslant w) = \mathrm{pr}\{\max(W_k + V_k, 0) \leqslant w\} = \mathrm{pr}(W_k + V_k \leqslant w)$$

$$= \int_{-\infty}^{\infty} \mathrm{pr}\{V_k \in (v, v+dv)\} \mathrm{pr}(W_k \leqslant w - v \mid V_k = v)$$

$$= \int_{-\infty}^{w} g(v) \, dv \, F_k(w-v)$$

since $\mathrm{pr}(W_k \leqslant w - v \mid V_k = v) = 0 \, (v > w)$ and using the independence of W_k and V_k,

As $k \to \infty$, $F_k(w) \to$ a limit $F(w)$ which satisfies

$$F(w) = \int_{-\infty}^{w} F(w-v) g(v) \, dv.$$

It can be shown that $F(w) = \mathrm{pr}(\sum_{k=1}^{n} V_k \leqslant w$ for all $n)$ $(w \geqslant 0)$; and if $\mathrm{E}V_k \geqslant 0$ then $F(w) \equiv 0$, i.e. the queue grows without limit; but if $\mathrm{E}V_k < 0$, then $F(w) \to 1$ as $w \to \infty$ so the limit $F(w)$ is a df.

Problem 7.10 *The busy period of a single-server queue with Poisson arrivals.* Suppose that customers join the queue at times which form a Poisson process of rate α, and that the service times are independent rvs having characteristic function $\psi(\theta)$. Find equations for the pgf $G(s)$ for N, the number of customers served during a busy period, and for the cf $\phi(\theta)$ for the busy period, B.

Solution. The starting times of the busy periods—that is, the time points when a customer arrives and can be served without waiting—are renewal points. The ends of the busy periods—that is, the time points when the server becomes idle—are also. The busy periods are therefore independently and identically distributed rvs.

The number, A, of customers who arrive during the service time, X, of the first customer, C_1, is $\mathscr{P}(\alpha X)$, so

$$\mathrm{E}_{A \mid X = x} s^A = \exp\{-\alpha x(1-s)\}$$

These customers are $C_2, C_3, \ldots, C_{A+1}$. Without losing generality we impose a *last-come first-served* queue discipline. Then C_{A+1} is served second. While C_{A+1} is being served, other customers arrive and will all be served before C_A. The number served starting with C_{A+1} before C_A is reached is a rv N_A distributed exactly like N, the number served in a busy period. Similarly, the number, N_{A-1}, served, starting with C_A, before C_{A-1} is reached is also distributed as N, and is independent of N_A. Therefore, given A,

$$N = 1 + N_1 + N_2 + \ldots + N_A$$

where the 1 is for C_1's service, so

$$\mathrm{E}_{N \mid A = a} s^N = s\{G(s)\}^a$$

83

Therefore

$$G(s) = \mathrm{E}_N s^N = \mathrm{E}_{X,A,N} s^N = s\,\mathrm{E}_X \mathrm{E}_{A|X=x}\{G(s)\}^A$$
$$= s\,\mathrm{E}_X \exp[-\alpha X\{1-G(s)\}] = s\,\psi[\mathrm{i}\alpha\{1-G(s)\}]$$

If $N = n$, then $B = X_1 + \ldots + X_n$, so, by equation 2.28,

$$\phi(\theta) = G\{\psi(\theta)\} = \psi(\theta)\psi[\mathrm{i}\alpha\{1-\phi(\theta)\}] \qquad \square$$

This problem can be formulated as a random walk and, as such, a special case was solved in Problems 5.7 and 5.8.

EXERCISES

1. *A paralysable counter.* A counter records the events of a Poisson process having parameter λ. After recording an event, the counter becomes locked for a fixed period γ, and will miss any events of the Poisson process which occur during that time. The intervals between recorded events are therefore independently distributed like an rv $X + \gamma$, where X is an $\mathscr{E}(\lambda)$ rv. By writing the time to the nth recorded event as

$$S_n = (X_1 + \gamma) + (X_2 + \gamma) + \ldots + (X_n + \gamma)$$

and using Exercises 15 and 16 of Chapter 2, and equation 7.1, prove that N_t, the number of recorded events in $(0, t)$ if an event was recorded at time 0 has distribution function

$$\mathrm{e}^{-\lambda(t-n\gamma)} \sum_{k=0}^{n-1} \frac{\{\lambda(t-n\gamma)\}^k}{k!}$$

2. Suppose that the locked periods of the paralysable counter are independent $\mathscr{E}(\rho)$ rvs. If the counter is initially unlocked and set to record the events of a Poisson process having parameter λ, show by a decomposition based on the final Δ, that p_t, the probability that the counter is locked at time t satisfies

$$\frac{dp_t}{dt} + (\rho + \lambda)p_t = \lambda$$

and obtain the solution.

3. Find the solution, $\Pi_t(s)$, of equation 7.5 in the special case in which the number of offspring of an individual is equally likely to be 0 or 2, and the lifetime distribution is $\mathscr{E}(2\alpha)$. What is the chance that the population is extinct by time t, if it starts at time 0 with the birth of a single individual?

4. *The linear birth and death process with immigration.* Show by a decomposition based on the arrival of the first immigrant that the pgf, $\Phi_t(s)$,

for the population size at time t, if initially there are no members of the population, satisfies

$$\Phi_t(s) = e^{-\alpha t} + \int_{u=0}^{t} \Pi_{t-u}(s)\Phi_{t-u}(s)\alpha e^{-\alpha u}\, du$$

where the immigration rate is α, and $\Pi_t(s)$ is the pgf for the process with no immigration from a single member given in Exercise 4 of Chapter 6. Solve this equation for $\Phi_t(s)$ and verify that the solution is that derived in Problem 6.3.

Show that as $t \to \infty$, if $\lambda < \mu$, the distribution of the population size becomes negative binomial with parameters α/λ and $1 - \lambda/\mu$.

5.   Consider the linear birth process with immigration, with n individuals present at time zero (Exercise 3 of Chapter 6). We can write the population size at time t, Z_t, in the form

$$Z_t = Y_t^{(1)} + \ldots + Y_t^{(n)} + X_t$$

where the $Y_t^{(j)}$ are independent pure birth processes from single individuals, independent of X_t, which is a linear birth process with immigration having no individuals present initially. Then the pgf for $Y_t^{(j)}$ is found by taking $f(u)$ to be an exponential density in Problem 7.7. Then, by a decomposition based on the time of arrival of the first immigrant, find the pgf for X_t. Hence find the pgf for Z_t.

6.   A secret society was started at time 0 by a single individual, the founder. In any short time interval $(t, t+\Delta)$ each member independently introduces a new member with probability $\lambda\Delta + o(\Delta)$. Members independently resign or die at a time after joining which is $\mathscr{E}(\mu)$. The founder, who never resigns, dies after the society has been running for a time which is $\mathscr{E}(\lambda - \mu)$, where $\lambda > \mu$. Derive, by a decomposition based on the admission of the first new member, the pgf for the membership size at time t, conditional on the founder still being alive then. Hence find the pgf for the membership size just after the founder's death.

7.   For the model of accident proneness described in Exercise 1 of Chapter 6, by means of a decomposition based on the time of the first accident, show that the pgf for the number of accidents in $(0, t)$ is

$$\{\alpha s e^{-\beta(1-s)t} - (\beta - \alpha)(1-s)e^{-\alpha t}\}/\{\beta s - (\beta - \alpha)\}.$$

Note that this reduces to the pgf for a Poisson rv when $\alpha = \beta$.

Chapter 8

Diffusion Processes

These are Markov processes $\{Z_i : t \in T\}$ having continuous time parameter spaces and continuous state spaces, and for which a small change in t results in only a small change in Z_t. A realisation can be thought of as being the path of a particle moving very erratically in a continuous medium, its progress depending only on its current position.

An important class of diffusion processes are the *Gaussian processes*. If $\{Z_t : t \in T\}$ is a process whose state space is the real line, R, and if its parameter space, T, is any subset of R, then it is a *Gaussian process* if, for every finite n, $(Z_{t_1}, \ldots, Z_{t_n})$ has a multivariate normal distribution. A Gaussian process is stationary if its covariance function $g(s, t) = g(t-s)$. The *Wiener* (or *Brownian motion*) process with parameter λ, $\{Z_t : t \in R\}$, is the Gaussian process with independent increments having $EZ_t = 0$ and $g(s, t) = \lambda \min(s, t)$, $(\lambda > 0)$.

Problem 8.1 If $\{Z_t\}$ is Wiener with parameter α, show that $\{Y_t\} = \{e^{-\lambda t} Z_{e^{2\lambda t}}\}$ is a stationary Gaussian process, and determine its covariance function, $g(s, t)$.

Solution. If Z_t is a normally distributed rv, then so is $a(t)Z_{b(t)}$, where a and b are real functions of t, since, for fixed t, $a(t)$ and $b(t)$ are real constants. The process $\{Y_t\}$ is therefore Gaussian, since Z_t is normal. Now

$$EY_t = e^{-\lambda t} EZ_{e^{2\lambda t}} = 0$$

since $EZ_t = 0$ for all t. Therefore

$$
\begin{aligned}
g(t, t+\tau) &= \operatorname{cov}(Y_t, Y_{t+\tau}) = E(Y_t Y_{t+\tau}) \\
&= E\{e^{-\lambda t} Z_{e^{2\lambda t}} e^{-\lambda(t+\tau)} Z_{e^{2\lambda(t+\tau)}}\} \\
&= e^{-\lambda(2t+\tau)} \operatorname{cov}\{Z_{e^{2\lambda t}}, Z_{e^{2\lambda(t+\tau)}}\} \\
&= \alpha e^{-\lambda(2t+\tau)} \min\{e^{2\lambda t}, e^{2\lambda(t+\tau)}\} = \alpha e^{-\lambda|\tau|}
\end{aligned}
$$

which does not depend on t. □

These processes can arise as the limit of a random walk. Let us consider again the unrestricted random walk, but suppose that the particle takes independent short steps of length Δx, to the right with probability p, and to the left with probability $q = 1-p$, after short time intervals of length Δt. It is a delicate matter how we let both Δx and Δt tend to zero.

During a time interval of length t, the displacement Z_t is approximately $t/\Delta t$ independent steps. Therefore, from equations 3.4,

$$\mathrm{E}Z_t \approx \frac{t}{\Delta t}(p-q)\Delta x = (p-q)t\frac{\Delta x}{\Delta t}$$

$$\mathrm{V}Z_t \approx \frac{t}{\Delta t}4pq(\Delta x)^2 = 4pqt\frac{(\Delta x)^2}{\Delta t}$$

If we let Δx and $\Delta t \to 0$ in such a way that $(\Delta x)^2/\Delta t \to \alpha$ and

$$p = \frac{1}{2}+\frac{\beta}{2\alpha}\Delta x, \qquad q = \frac{1}{2}-\frac{\beta}{2\alpha}\Delta x$$

where α and β are constants, then $\mathrm{E}Z_t \to \beta t$ and $\mathrm{V}Z_t \to \alpha t$. By the central limit theorem $(Z_t - \beta t)/\sqrt{(\alpha t)} \to$ an $\mathrm{N}(0,1)$ rv.

Problem 8.2 Show that $u_{x,t}$, where

$$u_{x,t}\,dx = \mathrm{pr}\{Z_t \in (x, x+dx)\}$$

satisfies the forward partial differential equation

$$\frac{\partial u}{\partial t} = -\beta\frac{\partial u}{\partial x} + \tfrac{1}{2}\alpha\frac{\partial^2 u}{\partial x^2}. \tag{8.1}$$

Solution. From equation 2.12, by a decomposition based on the last Δt,

$$\mathrm{pr}(Z_{t+\Delta t} = x) = \mathrm{pr}(Z_t = x-\Delta x)\mathrm{pr}(Z_{t+\Delta t} = x \mid Z_t = x-\Delta x)$$
$$+ \mathrm{pr}(Z_t = x+\Delta x)\mathrm{pr}(Z_{t+\Delta t} = x \mid Z_t = x+\Delta x)$$

Therefore

$$u_{x,t+\Delta t} = u_{x-\Delta x,t}\,p + u_{x+\Delta x,t}\,q.$$

We expand each term in a Taylor series up to $O(\Delta t)^2$ or $O(\Delta x)^3$, and abbreviate $u_{x,t}$ to u.

$$u_{x,t+\Delta t} = u+(\Delta t)\frac{\partial u}{\partial t}+O(\Delta t)^2$$

$$u_{x-\Delta x,t} = u+(-\Delta x)\frac{\partial u}{\partial x}+\tfrac{1}{2}(-\Delta x)^2\frac{\partial^2 u}{\partial x^2}+O(\Delta x)^3$$

$$u_{x+\Delta x,t} = u+(\Delta x)\frac{\partial u}{\partial x}+\tfrac{1}{2}(\Delta x)^2\frac{\partial^2 u}{\partial x^2}+O(\Delta x)^3$$

Then

$$u + (\Delta t) \frac{\partial u}{\partial t} + O(\Delta t)^2$$

$$= u(p+q) + (-p+q)(\Delta x) \frac{\partial u}{\partial x} + \tfrac{1}{2}(p+q)(\Delta x)^2 \frac{\partial^2 u}{\partial x^2} + O(\Delta x)^3$$

Now $p + q = 1$, $-p + q = -(\beta/\alpha)\Delta x$, therefore

$$\frac{\partial u}{\partial t} + O(\Delta t) = -\frac{\beta}{\alpha} \left\{ \frac{(\Delta x)^2}{\Delta t} \right\} \frac{\partial u}{\partial x} + \frac{1}{2} \left\{ \frac{(\Delta x)^2}{\Delta t} \right\} \frac{\partial^2 u}{\partial x^2} + O\left(\Delta x \frac{(\Delta x)^2}{\Delta t} \right)$$

Letting Δx and $\Delta t \to 0$ in such a way that $(\Delta x)^2/\Delta t \to \alpha$, we obtain equation 8.1.   □

Problem 8.3   Show that the Brownian motion process satisfies equation 8.1.

Solution. Here $EZ_t = 0$, so $\beta = 0$; and $VZ_t = \alpha \min(t, t) = \alpha t$. Therefore, since the displacement Z_t is $N(0, \alpha t)$, from equation 2.29 we have that

$$p_t(x, y)\, dy = \text{pr}\{Z_t \in (y, y+dy) \,|\, Z_0 = x\}$$

$$= \frac{1}{\sqrt{(2\pi\alpha t)}} \exp\left\{ -\frac{1}{2\alpha t}(y-x)^2 \right\} dy \quad (-\infty < y < \infty)$$

It is easy to check that $u_{y,t} = p_t(x, y)$ satisfies the standard diffusion equation

$$\frac{\partial u}{\partial t} = \tfrac{1}{2}\alpha \frac{\partial^2 u}{\partial y^2}$$ □

Often α and β will depend on x, but not on t. The forward equation, which is then known as the *Fokker–Planck* equation, is

$$\frac{\partial u}{\partial t} = -\frac{\partial}{\partial x}\{\beta(x)u\} + \frac{1}{2}\frac{\partial^2}{\partial x^2}\{\alpha(x)u\}$$

If, for a Markov chain $\{Z_n\}$, we evaluate the functions

$$\beta^*(k) = E_{Z_{n+1}|Z_n=k}(Z_{n+1} - Z_n) \quad \text{and} \quad \alpha^*(k) = V_{Z_{n+1}|Z_n=k}(Z_{n+1} - Z_n)$$

then we can easily approximate the chain by the corresponding diffusion process having $\beta(x) = \beta^*(x)$ and $\alpha(x) = \alpha^*(x)$.

Problem 8.4   *The Ehrenfest model of gas diffusion.* Find the diffusion limit of the Markov chain of Problem 4.11 if Δx, $\Delta t \to 0$ and $a \to \infty$ in such a way that

$$(\Delta x)^2/\Delta t \to \gamma, \qquad a\,\Delta t \to \beta^{-1}$$

Solution. Let $X_n^* = X_n - a$ and $k = i - a$. If $X_t^* = X_{n\Delta t}^* = k\Delta x = x$, say, then

$$X_{t+\Delta t}^* = X_{(n+1)\Delta t}^* = \begin{cases} (k+1)\Delta x = x + \Delta x \text{ with probability} \\ \qquad\qquad \tfrac{1}{2} - \tfrac{1}{2}k/a = \tfrac{1}{2}(1 - x/a\Delta x) \\ (k-1)\Delta x = x - \Delta x \text{ with probability} \\ \qquad\qquad \tfrac{1}{2} + \tfrac{1}{2}k/a = \tfrac{1}{2}(1 + x/a\Delta x) \end{cases}$$

Then

$$u_{x,t+\Delta t} = u_{x-\Delta x,t}\tfrac{1}{2}\{1 - (x - \Delta x)/a\Delta x)\} + u_{x+\Delta x,t}\tfrac{1}{2}\{1 + (x + \Delta x)/a\Delta x\}$$

i.e.

$$u + (\Delta t)\frac{\partial u}{\partial t} + O(\Delta t)^2$$

$$= \frac{1}{2}\left(1 + \frac{1}{a} - \frac{x}{a\Delta x}\right)\left\{u - (\Delta x)\frac{\partial u}{\partial x} + \tfrac{1}{2}(\Delta x)^2\frac{\partial^2 u}{\partial x^2} + O(\Delta x)^3\right\}$$

$$+ \frac{1}{2}\left(1 + \frac{1}{a} + \frac{x}{a\Delta x}\right)\left\{u + (\Delta x)\frac{\partial u}{\partial x} + \tfrac{1}{2}(\Delta x)^2\frac{\partial^2 u}{\partial x^2} + O(\Delta x)^3\right\}$$

$$= \left(1 + \frac{1}{a}\right)u + \tfrac{1}{2}(\Delta x)^2\frac{\partial^2 u}{\partial x^2} + \left(\frac{x}{a}\right)\left(\frac{\partial u}{\partial x}\right) + O(\Delta x)^3 + O((\Delta x)^2\Delta t)$$

Therefore

$$\frac{\partial u}{\partial t} + O(\Delta t) = \left(\frac{1}{a\Delta t}\right)\frac{\partial}{\partial x}(ux) + \frac{1}{2}\frac{(\Delta x)^2}{\Delta t}\left(\frac{\partial^2 u}{\partial x^2}\right) + O\left(\Delta x\frac{(\Delta x)^2}{\Delta t}\right) + O(\Delta x)^2$$

Therefore

$$\frac{\partial u}{\partial t} = \beta\frac{\partial}{\partial x}(ux) + \tfrac{1}{2}\gamma\frac{\partial^2 u}{\partial x^2} \qquad\qquad \square \quad (8.2)$$

This limiting equation is the diffusion equation for the *Ornstein–Uhlenbeck* process, which is defined to be the Gaussian process with $EZ_t = 0$ and covariance function $g(s,t) = \alpha e^{-\beta|s-t|}$ ($\alpha > 0$, $\beta > 0$). Problem 8.1 showed a method of constructing it from a Wiener process.

EXERCISES

1. If $\{X_t : t \in [0, \infty)\}$ is the Wiener process with parameter λ, for each

of the following processes $\{Z_t : t \in [0, \infty)\}$ find EZ_t, $\mathrm{cov}(Z_s, Z_t)$ $(s < t)$, and state whether the process is stationary in the wide sense, and whether it is Gaussian.

(i) $Z_t = \alpha t + X_t$ $(\alpha > 0)$,   (ii) $Z_t = X_{t+\tau} - X_t$ $(\tau > 0)$,

(iii) $Z_t = (1-t) X_{t/(1-t)}$ $(0 < t < 1)$, $Z_t = 0$ $(t \geqslant 1)$,

(iv) $Z_t = Y_{t+1} - Y_t$, where Y_t is Gaussian with

$$EY_t = \alpha + \beta t, \qquad \mathrm{cov}(Y_t, Y_{t+\tau}) = e^{-\gamma|\tau|} \quad (\gamma > 0)$$

2. Consider the diffusion limit of an unrestricted random walk on the real axis. If at time t, $X_t = x$, then at time $t + \Delta t$

$$X_{t+\Delta t} = X_{(n+1)\Delta t} = \begin{cases} (n-1)\Delta x = x - \Delta x & \text{with probability } p_x \\ n\Delta x = x & \text{with probability } r_x \\ (n+1)\Delta x = x + \Delta x & \text{with probability } p_x \end{cases}$$

where p_x and r_x are continuous functions of x, and $2p_x + r_x = 1$ for every value of x.

Let $u_{x,t}\, dx = \mathrm{pr}\{X_t \in (x, x+dx)\}$. If Δx and Δt both tend to zero in such a way that $(\Delta x)^2 / \Delta t \to \beta$, a constant, show that in the limit $u = u_{x,t}$ satisfies

$$\frac{\partial u}{\partial t} = \beta \frac{\partial^2}{\partial x^2}(p_x u)$$

3. Consider a particle which starts at the origin and carries out a random walk according to Problem 8.2. If $\phi_t(\theta)$ is the characteristic function for Z_t, and if $\psi(\theta)$ is the cf for a $N(\beta, \alpha)$ rv, show by a decomposition of $\phi_{t+\Delta t}(\theta)$ based on the last Δt that

$$\phi_t(\theta) = e^{\psi(\theta)t}$$

4. In a model for gas diffusion through a porous membrane there are 2 cells, A and B, each containing $2c$ molecules. These molecules are of 2 types: there are $2c$ black ones and $2c$ white ones. After each unit interval in time one molecule is chosen at random from each cell, and the 2 molecules are interchanged. The rv X_n is the number of black molecules in A at time n. Consider the Markov chain $\{Z_n : n = 0, 1, 2, \ldots\}$, where $Z_n = X_n - c$. Find difference equations in k and n for $p_k^{(n)} = \mathrm{pr}(Z_n = k)$ by a decomposition based on the last step.

Consider the diffusion process arising as follows. If at time instant t, $Z_t = z$, then at $t + \Delta t$, $Z_{t+\Delta t} = z - \Delta z$, z or $z + \Delta z$, where the process has state space $(-c, c)$. If both Δz and Δt tend to zero, and c tends to infinity in such a way that $(\Delta z)^2/\Delta t \to \gamma$ and $(c \Delta t)^{-1} \to \beta$, show that in the limit $u_{z,t}$ satisfies the Ornstein–Uhlenbeck process differential equation

$$\frac{\partial u}{\partial t} = \beta \frac{\partial}{\partial z}(zu) + \tfrac{1}{4}\gamma \frac{\partial^2 u}{\partial z^2}$$

where

$$u_{z,t}\, dz = \mathrm{pr}\{Z_t \in (z, z+dz)\}$$

5. Suppose that $\{Z_t : t \in [0, \infty)\}$ is the Ornstein–Uhlenbeck process. If Z_t given that $Z_0 = z$ is $\mathrm{N}\{ze^{-\beta t}, \gamma(1-e^{-2\beta t})/(2\beta)\}$, show that $u_{x,t}\mathrm{dx} = \mathrm{pr}\{Z_t \in (x, x+dx)\,|\,Z_0 = z\}$ satisfies equation 8.2. Note that the equilibrium distribution of Z_t is given by letting $t \to \infty$, and so is $\mathrm{N}(0, \gamma/2\beta)$, which does not depend on z.

Recommendations for Further Reading

A fairly elementary introduction to probability theory is volume 1 of *An Introduction to Probability Theory and its Applications* by William Feller, the third edition of which was published by John Wiley in 1968.

General treatments of stochastic processes at about the level of this Problem Solver are given in *The Theory of Stochastic Processes* by David R. Cox and Hilton D. Miller, published by Methuen in 1965, and in *The Elements of Stochastic Processes with Applications to the Natural Sciences* by Norman T. J. Bailey, published by John Wiley in 1964.

Some specific applications are made in *Queues* by David R. Cox and Walter L. Smith, published by Methuen in 1961, *The Theory of Storage* by P. A. P. Moran, published by Methuen in 1959, and *Stochastic Models for Social Processes* by David J. Bartholomew, the second edition of which was published by John Wiley in 1973.

Index

92